HAROLD WASHINGTON LIBRARY CENTER

R0022040995

W9-AYB-019

HD
8039
.S42   Cohn, Michael.
U617
        Black men of the sea

DATE			

BUSINESS/SCIENCE/TECHNOLOGY DIVISION

© THE BAKER & TAYLOR CO.

BLACK MEN OF THE SEA

BLACK MEN

OF THE SEA

by Michael Cohn and Michael K. H. Platzer

ILLUSTRATED WITH PHOTOGRAPHS

DODD, MEAD & COMPANY   NEW YORK

Copyright © 1978 by Michael Cohn and Michael K. H. Platzer
All rights reserved
No part of this book may be reproduced in any form
without permission in writing from the publisher
Printed in the United States of America

1 2 3 4 5 6 7 8 9 10

Library of Congress Cataloging in Publication Data

Cohn, Michael.
    Black men of the sea.

    Bibliography: p.
    Includes index.
    1. Afro-American seamen—History. I. Platzer,
Michael K. H., joint author. II. Title.
HD8039.S42U617   331.6′3′96073   78-4873
ISBN 0-396-07546-0

Acknowledgments

Many people have helped make this book possible by furnishing information and inspiration. First of all, we would like to thank the many sailors, ex-sailors, and fishermen who talked to us about their trade, the ports they sailed from, and their shipmates. We had the opportunity of sailing aboard the menhaden fishing boat *Tideland,* the trawler *Marlin,* and the clammer *Althea;* and we wish to thank Jim Kennedy of Seacoast Corporation, Captain Louis Ventafreddo, Captain Gosta Lovgren, and their crews for allowing us to experience the fishing trade instead of just reading about it. We wish to thank Jorge Pedro Barbosa, Captain John Costa, Captain Pedro Evora, John Gomes, Alberto Lopes, Arnaldo Mendes, Felix Monteiro, Armando Perry, Mario Rose, and Roy Teixeira for providing information about the Cape Verde packet trade.

Norman Brouwer, Robert Burgess, Don Hill, Vincent Ligouri, Don Meisner, Ted Miles, Gail Schneider, Gordon Thomas, and Oakes White spent a great deal of time giving their specialized knowledge in answer to our endless

questions. The encouragement and guidance of Peter Stanford, president of the National Maritime Historical Society
is greatly appreciated. Anna Rossi was indispensable for
her typing. Miriam Freedman proofread all the chapters
and made many constructive suggestions. We would like to
thank our editor, Allen Klots, for his encouragement and
confidence in the project.

The libraries of the Cape Ann Historical Society, Essex
Institute, Hampton Institute, Mariner's Museum, Nantucket Library, Newark Museum, Newport Historical Society, Mystic Seaport, New Bedford Whaling Museum,
New York Public Library, Sag Harbor Library, Schomburg Collection of the New York Public Library, South
Street Seaport, Peabody Museum (Salem), Staten Island Institute of Arts and Sciences, and Weeksville Historical Society were made available to us and helped us find obscure
photographs and manuscript sources.

Support and help in putting the individual parts into a
larger concept was provided by anthropologists, especially
Raoul Anderson, Peter Fricke, Esther Goldfrank, Laura
Houston, Estellie Smith, Ivan Van Sertima, A. Teixeira da
Mota, and Karl Wittfogel.

Georgette Gonsalves, high school teacher of Cape Verdean students, the staff of the Brooklyn Children's Museum, and Susan Cohn, encouraged, criticized, and served
as endless sounding boards while this project was in pro-
duction. We hope that young people as well as adults will
enjoy this book.

For mistakes of commission and omission, we hold our-
selves fully responsible.

MICHAEL COHN
MICHAEL K. H. PLATZER

Contents

Illustrations

Foreword

The heritage of black seafaring makes a proud and challenging chapter in our American experience at sea.

Michael Cohn of the Brooklyn Children's Museum and Michael Platzer of the United Nations in New York came together because of their interest in that heritage, which they had explored in separate experiences. For some years Michael Cohn had gone to sea with black menhaden men, dredged clams off New Jersey, and shared the experiences of the trawlers off New York bight—all trades carried on for centuries off our coasts. He learned the ways of life that these people followed in the disciplines of the fisheries.

Mr. Platzer fell in with the Cape Verdeans who came to our shores in packet ships that made their way across wide oceans under sail, preserving arts and skills long vanished from the sea. Thanks largely to his efforts, working with the National Maritime Historical Society, the *Ernestina/ Effie M. Morrissey,* last sailing packet in this trade, is now well on her way to being saved as a monument to this hardy voyaging. And thanks to the joint efforts of these authors, we have in this book a work we can share with joy. For the people whose lives they write of, people who wrest their living from the sea, have important things to tell us—whether the overflowing happiness when the community turns out to welcome a small ship sea-wracked from dangerous voyaging, or the sadness of loss when the sea claims its own. They are men, and what they have to tell us of our shared humanity makes their voyaging fresh and ever-memorable in these pages.

> PETER STANFORD, President
> *National Maritime Historical Society*

Preface

The black maritime heritage has been no different in many ways from that of any other ethnic or racial group—heroic exploits and voyages of discovery amid the more general experience of drudgery and exploitation for the common seamen. Yet the black seamen's experience is unique and worthy of separate examination. Their African origins and continuing contact with Africa made them different from other sailors.

One strong theme running through all the chapters of this book is that the black sea experience was more than a one-way trip between the decks of a dirty slave ship. There were a variety of maritime ties between America and Africa and regular two-way communication. American whalers stopped in Africa for crew, pirates settled in Madagascar and raided the Newfoundland fishing fleet; trading vessels manned by North American blacks continue to ply along the African coast, while sailing ships continuously brought immigrants from Africa as late as the 1960's.

Africa and Africans are not only part of our maritime

heritage, but Liberia, Ghana, Nigeria, and other African countries continue to play important roles in American maritime commerce. Nor is it possible to separate the West Indies from the North American mainland, for the sea connected the two instead of forming a barrier.

Blacks are an integral part of our maritime history. They served as sailors on all sorts of ships, went everywhere, and were as much at home on the sea as the saltiest New England Yankee. On the sea as on the land, however, they faced special problems and risks because they were black. The risk of re-enslavement, the restrictions of free black sailors in southern ports, and the fight against exclusion from certain job categories were unique to black sailors. The struggle for equality went on at sea as it did on land.

The sea gave blacks an opportunity to travel and to rise to positions of responsibility aboard ship, and these experiences altered their perceptions of themselves and their position in society. The subsequent fights for racial justice by Paul Cuffee, James Forten, Frederick Douglass, Robert Small, and Hugh Malzac were a direct result of their sea experiences. Blacks played a crucial role in the organization of the National Maritime Union, with its nondiscriminatory constitution. Black seamen in the U.S. Navy and Merchant Marine have been an important force in ending discrimination in the American armed forces and against blacks ashore.

However, not all of the blacks in these pages are heroes. There were black slavers and black pirates, as cruel as their white counterparts. But there were also brave fighters, great leaders, and many who simply endured while trying to make a good life and an adequate living. This book is mostly about ordinary men who toiled on the sea for a living. The harsh realities of "going to sea" make even the ordinary seaman's story heroic, for he had to struggle not only against the elements but often against discrimination. A black seaman was usually given the worst or most dangerous job until he proved himself.

The history of the black sailors and fishermen is not so much lost or stolen as it is strayed and scattered, for the people in some trades did not care about the skin color of their co-workers. For whalers, black skin was of no more importance than red hair; both were simply a form of identification on the crew lists or used as a basis for a nickname. In other cases, such as those of the coastal traders and the subsistence fishermen, records of any kind are scarce. The crew lists and the photographs taken toward the end of the whaling days, however, confirm the large role played by blacks in the whaling trade.

Many of the stories in this book came from the mouths of the people themselves, or from their children or grandchildren. Old whalers, captains of Cape Verde packets, deepwater sailors, and union organizers talked to us about the "old days." On board the menhaden fishing vessels, on sailing ships still operated in the West Indies and Africa by black men, and in the memories of seamen everywhere, the tremendous heritage of the black sailor and fisherman is still alive.

BLACK MEN OF THE SEA

You have crossed the seas
on whaling adventures
on those trips to America
from where ships sometimes never return

You have calloused hands
from pulling in the sheets
on those tiny sloops on the high seas;
You have survived horrible hours of anxiety
fighting against the storms;
You are tired and weary of the sea
and the endless long calms.

Under the infernal heat of the furnaces
you fed the boilers of the steamships with coal,
in peacetime
in wartime.
And you have loved with the sensual impulse of our people
women in foreign lands!
. . . .
These adventures across the oceans
no longer exist . . .
they only live
in the tales you recount of your past,
with a pipe hanging in your mouth
and with joyful laughter
that will never hide
your
melancholy. . .

From the Cape Verdean poem "Brother" by Jorge Pedro Barbosa

Translated by Jorge Pedro Barbosa and Michael K. H. Platzer

I

African Seafarers and Discoverers

Africans have a long, distinguished maritime heritage. The black pharaohs of Egypt are known to have sailed wooden plank ships 170 feet long on the Mediterranean and are believed to have reached American shores in the eighth century B.C. Thor Heyerdahl has proven that a papyrus boat built with the same techniques still employed in Chad today could have sailed across the Atlantic. The discovery of pre-Columbian negroid statues in America and the similarity of the pyramids, masonry, weaving, metalworking, use of purple, mummification, burial customs, calendars, and religion indicate there was contact between Nubian Egypt and Central America.

The Egyptian galleys were copied by the Phoenicians, Greeks, and Romans, while the reed boat of the Egyptians was imitated in the Far East. Nubian crews have been prized throughout the centuries by a number of nations. Egyptian ships are known to have visited the Somali coast, and there is an account of Necho II sending a ship from the Red Sea port of Ezion-Geber, down along the east coast of Africa, around the Cape of Good Hope, up the west coast, and through the straits of Gibraltar across the Mediterranean back to Egypt.

Before the birth of Christ the Azanians, who had migrated from Ethiopia and established communities along the East African coast, traded with the Mediterranean states via the Red Sea. Roman coins from the third century B.C. have been found in the area, and Egyptian records mention commerce with East Africa as early as the XIth Dynasty. A Greek account written in 50 A.D. mentions the "sewn" trading boats of East Africa. These *mtepe* appear to be completely African in origin and owe nothing to outside influences.

Before the sea-lanes from the Near East to Africa were taken over by the Persians, they were the trade route of the Sabeans—the tribe of the legendary King Prester John that was forced to retreat to the Ethiopian mountains following their conversion to Christianity in the fourth century. Sabean ships carried ivory, tortoiseshell, and rhinoceros horn from Africa; grain, wine, spears, knives, awls, urns, and trinkets from the Middle East to Africa; rice, yams, bananas, coconuts, betel, and sugarcane to East Africa from Southeast Asia; and cotton, sesame, castor beans, and sorghum to India. The Sabeans also introduced the dhow to East Africa, where they intermarried and settled.

Prosperous multiethnic city-states were developing at this time on the East African coast. The dynastic and religious feuds in Persia led to refugees from the province of Shiraz establishing the cities of Kilwa, Mombasa, Malindi, and Manda. The caliph of Damascus sent Syrian colonists to the Lamu archipelago and to Malindi, Mombasa, and Zanzibar in the seventh century; when he defeated the regents of Oman, they also fled to East Africa. At the same time, as a result of the wars among the Bantu in the Congo, more and more Negroes came or were brought to these trading centers to work in the plantations, shipyards, and on the ships of East Africa's developing cities.

Out of this intermingling arose the Swahili culture. The spectacular growth of the Swahili cities depended on their wide-ranging maritime commerce. The large dhows carried ivory, slaves, gold, carved wood, and rhinoceros horn as far afield as Malaysia. It is recorded that a Swahili prince shipped an elephant to the emperor of China as a gift in the thirteenth century, when gold flowed through Swahili cities to India.

When the Portuguese arrived in the fifteenth century they were surprised to see oceangoing sailing vessels and the sophisticated trading centers of the Swahili. Vasco da Gama lost no time sacking the Swahili coastal towns and placing the maritime trade under Portuguese control. However, the Swahili fought back and regained control of several of their city-states. The Portuguese then built Fort Jesus at Mombasa and went on to maintain control over the East African coast for more than two hundred years.

The Portuguese used Swahili sailors extensively aboard their ships. The Kilwa Chronicle relates that the Portuguese asked for a Swahili pilot to guide them to India. The Portuguese "discovery" of the sea route to India therefore was a simple feat with the aid of Swahili navigators who had traveled the Indian Ocean for centuries.

Columbus also relied on Africans to reach America. His pilot, Pedro Alonso Nino, was a North African, and his cabin boy was listed as Diego El Negro. African slaves completed the crew lists of most of the early Portuguese and Spanish ships. Africans were reported to be good seamen and performed useful services off the coast of Africa for the Europeans. Columbus had heard stories from Portuguese captains of African boats that started out from Guinea and navigated to the west to trade. Moreover, he found traces of Negro traders in America. He found handkerchiefs of cotton very symmetrically woven and worked in colors like those brought from Guinea and the gold spears of black traders of whom the Indians of Haiti spoke. Balboa actually ran into Africans in the Indies whom he believed had been shipwrecked. Negroid skeletons with the characteristic dental mutilation of early African cultures have been unearthed from graves dating from 1250 A.D. in the Virgin Islands. Terra-cotta pottery in pre-Columbia Central America shows negroid faces, and many words for trading items are similar in the West African Mandingo language and the native Mexican languages. The presence of distinctly African crops and of tobacco smoking in pre-Columbian America, and American maize in Africa, also indicates West African trader contact. A German doctor has proven that one can cross the Atlantic faster in an African dugout than Columbus did.

The story of Prince Abubakari II of Mali sending two expeditions across the Atlantic Ocean is confirmed by Arab records and by American Indian legends. This great Malian king had two hundred large boats built to be accompanied by two hundred supply boats filled with gold, items of trade, dried meat, preserved fruit, and other supplies to last two years. He told his captains not to return until they reached the end of the ocean, or when they exhausted their food and water. One ship returned, reporting that the others had found an ocean current that carried them swiftly out to sea. But this captain had been afraid to enter the current and had turned back. The king decided he must see for himself what lay on the other side of the ocean. He therefore organized a second fleet, larger than the first. He abdicated the throne to his brother and set sail with several hundred men and women across the Atlantic.

At approximately the same time, American Indian legends recount that a man in white robes with a black face and beard arrived from across the sea. West African cults and depictions of camels and African birds in America confirm the transatlantic crossing of a highly developed African civilization before the arrival of Europeans in the Western Hemisphere. Forty-six names of American Indian tribes appear to come directly from Africa.

The desert nomads of the Sahel and North Africa certainly had the knowledge and experience to navigate across vast expanses by means of the stars. The Koran states: "It is Allah who has appointed for you the stars, that ye guide yourselves thereby in the darkness of land and sea." The Arab-African seamen also had a primitive instrument known as a *kamal* to take readings of latitude. Moreover, ancient Arab maps indicate a western continent and therefore contact with America long before Columbus arrived.

The ancient dhows still ply their well-worn paths between Arabia, East Africa, and India. Navigating by changes in the color of the water, familiar landmarks, or dead reckoning, they cross thousands of miles of Indian Ocean. Most of the crews are Muslim Africans or Iranians, often descendants of African slaves. The conditions aboard these ships are as primitive as the navigation equipment, and are probably the same as they were a thousand years ago. The sailors continue to go to sea in these old ships because they know no other life; a son accompanies his father or uncle. Each crew member shares in the profits of a voyage, and most do a little personal smuggling on the side. They work hard, for they must load the cargo, sail the vessel, take care of the passengers, and solicit new business. The smaller coastal Lamu dhows are entirely run by Africans. The Swahili are also pilots in the ports of East Africa and are fishermen.

African Fishermen
and Traders

At dawn the fishermen of Guet N'Dar in Senegal leave their huts and go to the sea to launch their canoes as their forefathers have done for centuries. Fishing is one of man's earliest occupations, and coastal fishing was highly developed in Africa long before the arrival of the Europeans.

Although not as well known as either the Ghanians or the Somalis, the Wolof fishermen of Senegal are representative of the sophisticated social organization and courage required to undertake successful fishing. The West African coast is particularly treacherous due to shifting shoals, sandbars, and few sheltered harbors. During the dry season the trade winds blow from the north and northeast, often with storm force. During the wet season the rains are frequently accompanied by tornadoes, lightning, or violent gusts of wind. The hot, dry winds from the east will produce a hailstorm. After the rainy season there is almost always fog along the coast, especially in the morning and at dusk, caused by chilling of the water vapor by the colder beach sand. Throughout the year variable northwest winds usu-

ally rise in the afternoon and hinder navigation. Therefore
the fishermen leave very early and return before late afternoon.

The owner of a fishing boat usually gets up at five A.M.
and goes to the beach to observe the state of the sea. If he
thinks it is possible to go out, he wakes his crew—usually
members of his family or relatives. His son and young un-
married brother then carry the sail and spars down to the
boat while the captain finishes his breakfast of fish leftovers
mixed with rice from the night before. He then carries
down the lines, rudder, and bait and places them in the
boat, which is now ready to cross through the high surf.

Once the boat is launched, the crew—waist-high in the
water—try to hold it perpendicular to the ten-foot breakers,
which sometimes throw it back or drag it away. When the
surf looks manageable, the crew slide the boat forward,
jump in, and paddle furiously. Many of these frail skiffs
have been swamped, tipped over, and smashed by the
powerful breakers off the West African coast.

The skill of these West African fishermen was remarked
upon by the earliest European and American sea captains,
who relied upon the natives to get them ashore. Captain
Swan of Medford, Massachusetts, wrote in 1815 that he
was "conducted ashore by three naked negroes who paddle
the canoe standing up. They, however, manage dexterously
when in the surf. I have been many times off and on shore
in this way, but never without being wet through and often
upset. After landing on the beach to look on the tremendous sea that breaks upon it, our wonder is not that we
have got wet, but that the awkward thing that brought us
there ever reached it." In contrast to the native craft, the

rowboats dropped from European ships were usually "pitch-poled" end over end in the breakers and dashed on the beach, often drowning or breaking the limbs of those unaccustomed to the West African surf.

Having once passed the danger zone, the Wolof fishermen stow their paddles, step the mast, hoist the sail, and set out for the deep-sea fishing grounds. They take their bearings, for the low-lying coast disappears very quickly. After sailing for an hour or two, the captain orders the sail hauled down and the anchor stone, which had been stowed on the windward side to keep the boat balanced, thrown into the ocean, letting the line attached to it run for a moment, then fastening it to the seat.

During calmer months of the year, the fishermen kneel or sit on the seats in the canoe while fishing. When the catch is plentiful, the men stand up and are kept busy hauling in the surprisingly energetic fish, which can upset the boat at any moment. One fish, the *dyakhöfet*, which is popular with the tribes of the interior, is particularly formidable. This red fish is one meter in length and circumference and requires all the strength of the fishermen who are battling to bring it in. Even out of water the dyakhöfet remains dangerous, for his bite is ferocious; he is therefore killed immediately with a wooden club. Using a pointed piece of wood as a needle, the fishermen string the caught fish on a cord that is then tied to a seat. Under good conditions the boat may be full in an hour. However, in the foggy rainy season the Wolof fishermen usually start back before noon. Only the young and foolhardy will stay out until dusk or overnight in an open boat.

Sometimes the Wolof fishermen encounter sea turtles, a

prized delicacy. The fishing boat approaches the turtle very cautiously, as quietly as possible, while one of the fishermen, with his clothes off, stands ready. He jumps on the back of the turtle and seizes the sides of its shell with his hands, staying out of reach of its bite. The turtle starts to dive, but the naked rider leans backward, forcing the turtle to rise to the surface. When the fishing boat comes alongside, the animal is grabbed by its flippers and made fast upside down in the boat.

On the return trip the series of dangerous breakers must again be overcome. The sail is taken down and stowed shortly before reaching the shoals, and the paddles are taken out. The crew must hold the boat straight as it is carried rapidly to shore. Usually it is grounded on the sand of the beach, and then pulled beyond reach of the tides with the assistance of willing helpers on shore. The catch is entrusted to the wives of the fishermen. A few fish are kept for cooking and for gifts to relatives, and some are given to the helpers who moved the boat to its proper place. Another portion (the *saku*) is sold by the sister of the captain to pay for repairs to the boat and to provide for emergencies. The bulk of the catch is preserved or sold. The fish to be sold are washed by the women, placed in calabashes, and carried to a nearby market. Those to be preserved are eviscerated and dried in the sun. After two days these fish are sufficiently preserved to be transported to the interior of the country for sale there.

Because the men are so long absent at sea, the women play a prominent role in the economy of fishing societies. They fish in the rivers, grow crops, dye cloth, and sell their wares in the market. These women are allowed to retain a nest egg, which they can dispose of freely. If a man is lost at sea, the widow is taken care of by his family.

The women also have an important role in the opening of the fishing season. With the help of young girls, the sister of the oldest captain still able to sail prepares a liquid of millet mixed with couscous and honey and then curdled. The next day she gives it to the religious leader in a new gourd. This *marabout* in turn presents it to the crew of the first boat to leave. Not before this is done do the men go out to sea. A similar ritual takes place to prevent drownings and accidents on the river.

Fishing on the river, although less dangerous, reveals the cooperative spirit of the African community. A voluntary association of three or four river canoes work together to trap the fish when they are running. A fishing captain is selected by the community to organize the expedition. The women and children hold the nets while the men drive the schools of fish into the trap. The catch is divided by the approximate number of members of the association whether active or not (old men, women, and children of a certain age can belong to it), plus a unit for each boat in use. The share for the old men and the children is set aside first, then comes the share of the fishing captain, who gets the best quality fish as compensation.

It is impressive that there are no disputes over the distribution of the fish. There is a legend that a wise man, Ahmadou, showed the people how to cooperate so they could catch more fish; since then, all have accepted the precise rules of distribution.

Trading and marketing of fish and other goods were relatively sophisticated in Africa before the Europeans

came. Large trading canoes were observed in the fifteenth
century with fifty to one hundred paddlers. The canoes
carried fish, salt, and pottery up the rivers and brought
back agricultural products, meat, and slaves.

Separate villages were established by families engaged in
trading along the coast. They organized themselves into
efficient corporate enterprises, with each family member
having a specific function. Authority within the village was
vested in the founder and the elders, who acted as a consul-
tative council. It was unusual for the head of these trading
villages to make decisions entirely on his own; all the villagers had a common interest in promoting the trade of
their settlements.

The trading expeditions into the interior were often entrusted to slaves who returned faithfully. The entire system was based on trust, for the traders sent goods off without knowing whether the harvest was satisfactory or
products were available in the interior. Merchandise was
often left without payment, and debts were collected on a
later trip. A form of credit existed where children and
slaves were often taken as surety and returned upon payment of the debt.

Slavery, as practiced before the arrival of Europeans, was
a completely different institution from that practiced in
America. The lot of the slaves kept by the trading houses
was an accepted one, for they were completely relied
upon by the traders and in fact were later used to collect
slaves for the Europeans. The slaves of the trading societies,
who were highly prized for their ability to cross the surf
with trading goods, were often hired out to the European
captains.

The most famous of the African tribes who served the Europeans were the Krumen. Horatio Bridge, an officer in the United States Navy, wrote in 1848: "The Krumen are indispensable in carrying on the commerce and maritime business of the African coast. When the Krumen come alongside, you may buy the canoe, hire the men at a moment's warning and retain them in your service for months. They have no equipment save a piece of white or colored cotton girded about their loins. When rowing a boat or paddling a canoe, it is their custom to sing. . . . One of their number leads in recitative and the whole company respond in chorus. The subject of the song is a recital of the exploits of the men, their employments, their intended movements, the news of the coast and the character of their employers."

The British especially valued these African seamen, and many captains preferred them to white sailors. They were praised highly for their great industry, patience, intelligence, fidelity, and obedience. Although most came originally from Liberia, they were found at every trading place on the coast from Gambia to the Equator and on board every British vessel whether merchant or man of war. According to Bridge they were fun-loving, and Krumen attached to a man of war would taunt their friends aboard merchant vessels. Their main objective in entering the maritime service of the Europeans was to obtain the means to purchase wives back home and to retire to an easy life. Whenever a seaman returned, a bullock was killed and a feast was held.

The political organization of the Krumen was highly developed, and the community leaders could be removed by

popular will. Kru chiefs secured immunity from seaborne
slavery for their tribes by prearrangement with the European slave hunters. Distinguishing marks were cut on their
faces to indicate they were Kru and were to be left alone.

Because of their trading and maritime abilities, the
other coastal tribes were either co-opted into the slave trade
or were destroyed by the Europeans. The Itsekiri, primarily fishermen and suppliers of fish, salt, and crayfish to
the hinterland, became the great middlemen traders of
Benin when the Portuguese arrived. First they traded slaves
and then palm oil, which required even greater organization and "trust." Not only did the European merchants
have to entrust goods to the Itsekiri trading houses, but the
Itsekiri had to leave goods with the producers of the palm
oil. The Itsekiri traders maintained a large fleet of trading
canoes manned by slaves to collect and protect the oil from
seizure by other tribes. They also widened the creeks for
the large canoes and established a network of trading de-
pots. Some canoes carried forty paddlers and one hundred
fighting men. Nana, the leading merchant of Benin, at the
end of the nineteenth century had two hundred trade canoes, one hundred war canoes, and twenty thousand "boys"
who worked for him. In the 1880's a group of Nigerian
merchants were negotiating with a Liverpool concern for
the purchase of a steamer to sell their goods directly in
England. However, such independent commercial power—
the Itsekiri often refused to sell their oil if they felt the
price was too low—was not to be tolerated by the British,
who were establishing their own trading companies and
wished to obtain effective control over the interior. In
1894 Nana was arrested and his power broken; direct eco-

nomic exploitation by the British companies began. Although a few Africans participated in the English, French, and German trading corporations as middlemen, they were not again to play a major role in the shipping and external trading companies until the independence of the African colonies.

Today most African coastal nations are developing their ports, merchant marines, and fishing fleets, often with the cooperation of American or European concerns. Sierra Leone has a partnership with an American firm for tuna and shrimp fishing and with a Norwegian shipping company to provide employment for the large pool of experienced Sierra Leonean seamen. Ghananian fishermen have modernized their fishing techniques and taken over much of the artisanal fishing of West Africa. At the same time, Ghana established the first maritime officer training school in Africa and sends its graduates to complete their training in England or the United States. Nigeria is feverishly expanding its port capacities and fleet and is sending trainees to American merchant marine academies and engineering schools. The Kru sailors of Liberia are still very much in demand on all foreign ships. In 1947 Liberia admitted to her registry the American Farrell Line, which had been shipping along the West African coast employing Liberian crews for years. Subsequently, American oil companies began registering their tankers under the Liberian flag, and an intimate maritime partnership with Liberia developed.

III

The Slave Trade

In August 1839 a black schooner with tattered sails and apparently only Africans aboard was sighted off Long Island. A New York pilot boat and a New Bedford schooner offered to tow her to port, but when the black men brandished cutlasses, they cast her off again. Finally a brig of the U.S. Coast Guard was sent to investigate this suspicious ship. As they boarded the schooner, the leader of the Africans leaped over the side, naked except for his splendid necklace. A Coast Guard rowboat was immediately sent after him, but whenever it came near him, he would dive and surface some distance away. For an hour they chased him; finally exhausted, he allowed himself to be captured but first threw off his gold necklace and let it sink into the ocean. This was Cinque, leader of the slave uprising aboard the slaveship *Amistad,* which was to become a cause célèbre of the abolitionists and create international complications for four American presidents. The *New Haven Daily Herald* headlined a story of the rumored murder of twenty-six white men, women, and children

aboard the *Amistad:* "The Pirate Taken." Another newspaper, sympathetic to the slaves who revolted after endur-
ing two months in the hellhole of a slave ship without sufficient food and water, wrote: "This Cenquez is one of the
spirits who appear but seldom. Possessing far more sagacity
and courage than his race generally do, he had been ac-
customed to command. . . . His general deportment is free
from levity and many white men might take a lesson in
dignity and forebearance from the African Chieftain."

The slaves had been taken from Africa several months
before, had endured the grueling "middle passage," and
had then been transshipped to the *Amistad* in Cuba. Conditions aboard the ship worsened. Slaves were literally dying
of thirst, and when one asked for extra water, he was severely flogged. When they pleaded for more food (a single
plantain, some bread, and a cup of water was their daily
ration), they were told by the mulatto cook that they would
have their throats cut and be eaten by the whites. The
slaves aboard the *Amistad* held a council. One of them
later recounted (after they had learned some English),
"We feel bad, and we ask Cinque what to do. Cinque say,
'Me think and by and by I tell you.' Cinque then said, 'If
we do nothing, we be killed. We may as well die in trying
to be free as to be killed and eaten.' "

Cinque had found and hidden a nail. He waited for the
appropriate moment, then used the nail to undo the chain
that fastened them all to the wall and to each other. Freed,
they armed themselves with knives that they found in the
hold, crept on deck, and in the fog killed the cook and the
captain, who was at the wheel. Two other white sailors
jumped overboard, but Cinque spared the others for he

needed someone to sail the ship back to Africa. The Spanish owners begged not to be put in chains, but Cinque said, "You say fetters good for Negro, good for Spanish man, too; you try them two days and see how they feel." After two days Cinque gave them as much food and water as could be spared. In fact, when water was short Cinque would not drink and he urged the men to abstain, but he kept a little water for the children and for the Spaniards. The Spaniards, however, tricked Cinque, who knew Africa lay east. During the day the Spaniards sailed the schooner east, but at night turned her north, hoping to hit the eastern coast of the United States. When they sighted land (Long Island), Cinque went ashore to seek food.

He encountered two sea captains in Sag Harbor. By sign language and a few key words such as "America" and "Africa" he offered them all the gold aboard the ship if they would take the blacks back to Africa. The captains, who intended to take the schooner into Sag Harbor and claim salvage rights to her and all the cargo, were greatly disappointed when the Coast Guard appeared.

When the Coast Guard boarded the *Amistad* they found the Africans "in a state of nudity, emaciated to mere skeletons, coiled upon the decks" dying of hunger and thirst. Although they came from different tribes, Cinque was concerned for the welfare of each. As the "leader of the rebellion," he was put in irons and separately jailed. The others became demoralized and three died, so Cinque was allowed to rejoin the group.

Support for the Africans came almost immediately, for abolitionists had been looking for just such a case to get the United States Government to help abolish the slave trade. Thousands came to see the victims of Spanish slavery, and many brought them clothing and food. The Africans were first held in New Haven, and the Yale Divinity School took on the project to Christianize them and to send them back to Africa as missionaries. The best lawyers were recruited. Although the lower courts freed Cinque and his conspirators, the Spanish government insisted they be returned or paid for. Former President John Adams then took the case to the Supreme Court, whereupon the Africans were finally set free and returned to Sierra Leone. The *Amistad* committee later became the American Missionary Association, which established the Negro colleges of Hampton, Talladega, LeMoyne Dillard, Tougaloo, Huston-Tillotson, Atlanta, Fisk, and Howard. The *Amistad* affair aroused the anger of many Americans to the continued existence of the slave trade and led indirectly to the creation of Liberia and of a U.S.-Britain naval squadron to seize slavers.

Revolts aboard slaveships were not infrequent. One slaver recounted that there was always trouble with a particular African tribe. "Sometimes we meet with stout stubborn people amongst them, who are never to be made easy; and these are generally some of the Cormantines, a Nation of the Gold Coast. . . . We are obliged to secure them very well in irons, and watch them narrowly: yet they nevertheless mutinied, tho' they had little prospect of succeeding." Not only were they kept in irons and carefully watched, but they were fed only enough to keep them alive. The inhumane conditions aboard slaveships are well documented; however, the degree to which the slavers went to intimidate the slaves is less well known. One leader of an insurrection

was hung in front of the other slaves, shot ten times, de-
capitated, and the body left on deck "in order to prevent
further mischief."

Other times blacks were obliged to do the dirty work for
the white sea captains. A slaver recounted, "We have some
30 or 40 gold coast negroes, which we buy . . . to make
guardians and overseers of the Whidaw negroes, and sleep
among them to keep them from quarreling; and in order
as well to give us notice, if they can discover any caballing
or plotting among them which we trust they will discharge
with great diligence; when we constitute a guardian, we
give him a cat of nine tails as a badge of his office, which he
is not a little proud of, and will execute with great authority." Krumen were regularly hired as overseers. They reported to the captain any sign of insurrection and mer-
cilessly whipped anyone who threatened their authority.
"One morning a Kruman reported to the Spanish captain
a negro who had resisted his authority during the night.
The offender was hustled upon deck, stretched out at full
length, face downward, and tied to the ring-bolts. One of
the Krumen now commenced lashing the poor creature
over the back and when he flagged, another took his place
and renewed the beating. The Negro was grit to the bone
and made not the slightest outcry. Not until life was almost extinct did the Spaniard order him released." Another
incident of excessive punishment involving Krumen
aboard a Spanish slaver made even the crew think the
Spanish owner had gone too far:

The culprit was now brought before him when he gave
order to the Krumen to lash him to the ring-bolts in the

deck. After securing the poor wretch so that it would be impossible for him to move a limb, the order was given to the Krumen to proceed to business. This they did by beating him with their whips, putting forth all their strength in delivering the blows. The punishment continued so long that I thought the man would have died under it; but his endurance was wonderful and he only uttered a few groans. When the beating was finally discontinued, the Spaniard stooped down alongside of him and taking a razor out of his pocket, opened it and cut long, straight gashes in the flesh. Afterward, he took a flat piece of wood, resembling a ruler, and beat gently all around the wound which had the effect of making them bleed freely. Having accomplished this, he ordered the "shikko" [the negro in charge of the others] to get a pot full of brine out of the harness cask and apply it to the bleeding wounds. When this was done, the poor negro could suppress his anguish no longer and groaned aloud. After being kept in this awful agony for ten minutes, he was released from the ring-bolts and put in double irons.

On another ship the slaves succeeded in bashing in the head of the mulatto overseer and in liberating several dozen slaves before the other Negro guards shot thirteen of them and broke the rebellion. Some of the slave revolts were successful, especially if the boats were still off the coast of Africa. Once a Dutch ship full of slaves was preparing to set sail, but ill treatment by the captain so aroused the slaves that they set upon the ship's crew and took possession of the vessel. Often the slaves were recaptured by African slave traders or privateers. Many liberated slaveships foundered in the Atlantic because the Africans had killed the whites aboard and were inexperienced in sailing and keeping a course.

Mutineers safely brought other ships to British possessions where slavery had been abolished. The successful
slave revolt aboard the *Creole* created a great strain in
relations between the United States and Great Britain.
Led by a runaway slave, Madison Washington, the slaves
completely surprised the crew of the *Creole,* which had left
Richmond for New Orleans with a slave cargo. One white
man was killed and the rest placed in chains. A musket
doubly charged was held at the first mate's breast to ensure he would take the brig to a British port. After they
arrived in Nassau, the U.S. Government demanded the
return of these "murderers and pirates," but the British
government refused.

The relationship between the white crew and the slaves
was not always antagonistic. During the British Parliament
hearings on the abolition of the slave trade, many sea captains swore the slaves were well treated aboard ship. While
most of their claims of providing sufficient food, space, and
even entertainment were patent lies, it is true that they
could only make money if they brought their cargo over
alive. A song was sung by the slaves in Jamaica in honor
of Captain Hugh Crow, one of the last British slavers, for
his good treatment of the slaves while aboard ship. He
taught them to work the vessel and to fire the guns to protect the ship. Once off Tobago twelve slaves died defending the ship against a French privateer. Mungo Park related another incident where the Africans were taken
out of irons to work the pumps so the vessel would not
sink. Some slaves proved to be good sailors and were kept
by the captain of the ship or were sold as apprentice seamen. On some slavers one third of the crew was black.

The condition of the sailor aboard a slaver was often worse than that of a slave. A former slave recounted of his voyage, "I had never seen among my people such instances of brutal cruelty and this not only shown towards us blacks but also to some of the whites themselves." A sailor was flogged to death because he refused his captain's black mistress the keys to the wine locker. The abolitionists in England established that there was a higher death rate among sailors than among slaves. The sailor usually had also been kidnapped, but rather than bringing a good price at the end of the voyage he had to be paid. Therefore a captain would frequently make conditions so bad that they would desert in the first port in the Caribbean—sailors who deserted before the voyage was over were forced to work in chains when caught.

Water was limited aboard ship, and a sailor's daily ration was one quart. In the equatorial climate this would not be sufficient to quench his thirst. To survive, seamen would lick the dew off the gunwales in the morning. The water on the African coast was malaria-infested, and many sailors became ill or blind when they went ashore to refresh themselves. A cruel captain would leave his sick crew behind, for "dead sailors don't collect wages."

The slave ships carried small crews and they were worked hard. The crew had no quarters of their own and were obliged to sleep on deck when it stormed; they often stole down the hatchway to sleep with the slaves in the stinking hold. They not only had to care for the ship but also take care of the slaves and clean the filthy hold when the slaves were brought on deck. They were driven hard by ruthless captains interested only in delivering their cargo as fast as possible and maximizing their profit. The ships were often overloaded and unsafe. Diseases contracted in Africa would often take their toll of the entire crew, and the ship would founder. There are regular reports of the slaves sharing their rations with the starving crewmen. There were also instances of crew members delivering the slaves to freedom if the captain died. The crew of the *Elizabeth* refused to hand over the slaves to the captain of another of the owner's vessels. After being bribed with better wages and then threatened, the crew remained steadfast. The ship's cooper informed the other captain that the slaves had been on board a long time and that a great friendship had developed; the crew would therefore help them.

While slavery was accepted, the respected merchant families of New England, such as the Browns of Rhode Island, engaged in the slave trade. In 1708 Governor Cranston of Rhode Island reported that 103 vessels had been built in that tiny province between 1698 and 1708 and "in most cases made a slave voyage." The *Mayflower,* immediately after transporting the Pilgrims, was used to take the Negro slaves to the West Indies. Fifty-nine ships registered in Rhode Island and as many from Massachusetts entered the port of Charleston with slaves during the three years ending December 31, 1807. "Massachusetts is a state more responsible under heaven than any other community in this land for the introduction of slavery into the continent, with all the curses that have followed it," a citizen of North Carolina once accused. The first American-built slaver was the *Desire,* built at Marblehead, Massachusetts, in 1636; it returned to Boston in 1638 with a cargo of Negro slaves. Even after the abolition of the slave trade, the merchants of Salem still engaged in transporting slaves. The African Squadron, established by the U.S. Government to suppress the slave trade, reported in 1860, "The clipper ship *Nightingale* of Salem shipped a cargo of 2,000 negroes and has gone clear with them. . . . She is a powerful clipper and is the property of the captain, Bowen, who is called the Prince of Slaves." In 1861 she was seized by the U.S. sloop-of-war *Saratoga,* whose captain reported:

> For some time the American ship *Nightingale* of Boston, Francis Bowen, master, has been watched on this coast under the suspicion of being engaged in the slave trade. Several times we have fallen in with her and although fully assured that she was about to engage in this illicit trade she has had the benefit of the doubt. A few days ago observing her at anchor at Kabenda, I came in and boarded her and was induced to believe she was then preparing to receive slaves. Under this impression the ship was got under way and went some distance off but with the intention of returning under the cover of the night; which was done and at 10 P.M. we anchored and sent two boats under Lieutenant Guthrie to surprise her and it was found that she had 961 slaves on board and was expecting more. Lieut. Guthrie took possession of her as a prize and I have directed him to take her to New York. She is a clipper of 1,000 tons and has *Nightingale* of Boston on her stern and flies American colors.

As late as 1862 it was the fate of a New England sea captain, a native of Portland, to pay the extreme penalty for slave trading. In the summer of 1860 Captain Nathaniel Gordon, master of the *Erie,* sailed from New York for the Cayo River, where he took aboard 890 Negroes, 600 of whom were boys and girls, and "thrust them, densely crowded, between the decks and immediately set sail." The *Erie* was seized by the African Squadron and Gordon was brought to trial as a pirate, under the 1820 law that made slave trading an act of piracy. After two trials he was convicted and hanged on February 21, 1862.

Nonetheless the slave trade continued, particularly to Brazil. Portugal was the last nation to forbid its sea captains to engage in such trade. Portuguese mulattos remained active selling and transporting slaves until the end of the nineteenth century. A Cape Verdean captain, Quirino Pinheiro, is said to have brought hundreds of slaves to America. Francisco Feliz ("Cha-Cha") da Souza, a Brazilian of mixed blood who deserted the crew of a slaver, became the last famous "mongo" or slave trader on the West Coast of Africa. Once a community of black Portuguese established near the mouth of the Sierra Leone seized the slave cargo of a New England merchant and sold them themselves. There came to be an automatic prejudice that Portuguese-speaking seamen were either slavers or pirates. A group of colorfully dressed Portuguese seamen who landed in Sag Harbor in 1853 were immediately suspected of being slavers and had to escape across Long Island Sound from the local police.

At the end of the slave trade the slavers became desperados. Slaving was universally outlawed as piracy, and slavers boldly fought off the slow-moving British frigates sent to stop them. One slaver not only destroyed two war sloops—of the newly formed navy of Sierra Leone—but enslaved their Negro crews and sold them in the West Indies.

Blacks also served with distinction aboard the British warships, where they were compared favorably with English seamen. They thus played an active role in putting an end to the slave trade to the Americas. Afraid of disembarking in the United States, especially after the war of 1812, many black British sailors settled in Canada, where they became well-known as seamen and fishermen, shipping out of Nova Scotia.

IV

Pirates and Privateers

Whether slave trading, piracy, and privateering were respectable trades or despicable crimes depended on international politics and the social climate of the times in which they were taking place.

On March 11, 1835, Antonio Farrer, a native of Africa, was hanged in Boston, Massachusetts, for piracy. His death and that of his six Spanish and mulatto shipmates marked the end of a 250-year era of private armed vessels fighting on the ocean for their private profit.

Farrer was one of the crew members of the Baltimore clipper-schooner *Pinda,* which had sailed from Cuba. On September 21, 1832, she encountered the American brig *Mexican* sailing from Salem, Massachusetts, to Rio de Janeiro. Hoisting Colombian colors, the *Pinda* ran out her guns and ordered the Americans to heave to. The pirate-privateer then stripped the *Mexican* of valuables and set her afire. The fire was extinguished as soon as the *Pinda* was out of sight. When the *Mexican* returned to Salem she had the description of her opponent published in the

Essex Register: "A black Baltimore clipper with a white stripe, large gun on a pivot and brass 12 pounders gleaming in her side . . . about 70 men who appeared to be chiefly Spanish and mulatto."

This description was used by Captain Hunt of the American ship *Gleaner* to spot the *Pinda* in the harbor of Saint Thomas, an island off the coast of West Africa. He notified a British frigate, and the *Pinda* was pursued to the coast of Africa by the *Curlew,* a British brig-of-war. The crew of the *Pinda* tried to escape and seek refuge among the African tribesmen but were turned over to the British, who brought them to Salem for trial on August 27, 1834. Five of the crew were acquitted, one became insane, and six were hung.

Piracy and privateering had been a risky but profitable business in the Caribbean and off the African coast ever since the days of the Spanish galleons. In 1568 John Hawkins, an Englishman, was illegally selling black slaves to the Spanish when he was attacked by a Spanish fleet in the harbor of St. John de Ullua in Mexico. Since Hawkins had negotiated a truce with the Spanish commander, he accused them of breaking faith; the Spanish justified themselves by accusing him of piracy. By today's standards he would probably be called a smuggler. Despite his smuggling and slave dealing he became a folk hero and a knight when he returned to England. His coat of arms included a black in chains; it could have served as a coat of arms for many of the English filibusters. (The words "filibuster," "buccaneer," "corsair," "freebooter," and "pirate" were used interchangeably for those seamen operating for their private profit, with or without unofficial government approval.)

Francis Drake was an exception in this group. He made allies of the escaped blacks of the isthmus of Panama when he raided Nombre de Dios, and he did not deal in slaves. John Oxenham, another British sea dog, tried to imitate Drake. He too enlisted the blacks, called Cimarrons, but broke his agreement with them. Because of this the blacks turned against the pirates and joined the Spanish to destroy Oxenham. In the published accounts of this affair, the Spanish blame the Negroes for their initial defeat and the English blame the blacks for their "betrayal."

In 1603 Elizabeth of England died. Her successor, James I, had no use for the freebooters and proceeded to hang some of them for piracy. The rest did not stop their operations but shifted their base from England to North Africa. Under Sir John Mainwaring and others they operated out of Tripoli and Morocco in conjunction with the native African pirates. Since the fall of Constantinople in 1453 and the destruction of Rhodes in 1522, the North African fleets had reigned supreme in the Mediterranean. The defeat of the united Turkish and African fleets at Lepanto in 1571 turned the ships of Tunis, Algiers, and Tripoli from agents of Turkish expansion to out-and-out pirates. The coming of the British freebooters simply expanded their area of action. Ships with mixed British and African crews raided the fishing fleet off Newfoundland, harried the Spanish, Italian, and Maltese coasts, and fought the ships of all nations that did not pay tribute to the North African pirate states. Poor captives were sold as slaves while wealthier prisoners could be ransomed by their relatives. One of the more spectacular long-distance raids was on Iceland by Moroccan ships. The captives taken there were ransomed by the king of Denmark, but there is no record of any ransoming of the captives taken from the Newfoundland fishing fleet.

Caribbean piracy flourished at the same time as that of North Africa, and some individuals seem to have participated in both. French and English buccaneers seized the island of Tortuga, off Haiti, as a base and organized themselves as "Brethren of the Main." Some of the buccaneers had been "boucan" hunters, producers of smoked beef from wild cattle—hence the name "boucaneer"—but all of them became pirates as the occasion offered. When the English seized Jamaica from the Spanish in 1655, the English pirates made that island their base and marketplace instead of Tortuga. Officially, Jamaica was British territory as Tortuga was French. The "Royal Tenth" sent from Jamaica to London as the proceeds from the Jamaica court of admiralty amounted to as much as 50,000 pounds sterling a year, so officials naturally turned a blind eye to some of the unlawful activities of the privateers.

This piracy involved the welfare of the blacks living in the Caribbean area. Most of them fought on the side of the Spanish, not the pirates. Sir Henry Morgan, pirate and later governor of Jamaica, is recorded as having killed all the blacks who opposed him at Maracaibo, on the way to Panama, and in Panama itself. The hangman sent to finish off the French pirate L'Ollonais was a black. The scales of pay of buccaneer ships rated slaves at one hundred pieces of eight each, and it seems that many of the pirates dabbled in the slave trade. Certainly there was

little consideration paid to any captured black by these
fighters for "freedom from Spanish aggression." The blacks
who escaped from Spanish slavery took to the jungle instead of the sea and established colonies in Brazil, Guyana,
and Jamaica.

Although the pirates of the Caribbean occasionally took
a role in the wars of their mother country, they usually did
so as mercenaries, being promised a share of the loot of the
specific operations for which they were hired. Pirates did
not tackle ships of their own country, since many of the
pirate-captains eventually hoped to settle down as wealthy
squires at home after their retirement from piracy. Most
of the crews had no such ambitions and spent their money
as fast as they got it. Some of this gold flowed into the
pockets of blacks established as innkeepers and brothel
keepers on Jamaica and elsewhere.

In the 1680's a general peace in Europe permitted the
Spanish to make it unprofitable for the pirate frater-
nity to operate in the Caribbean. The pirates shifted
their base to Madagascar, off the east coast of Africa. From
there they raided ships traveling from India to Europe and
Arabia. The French pirate Mission, with the help of an
Italian priest and Captain Robert Tew of Rhode Island,
founded the settlement of "Libertatia" on Madagascar.
Mission was an idealist and early socialist, and his settlement allowed no distinction on the grounds of color or
race, and no slavery. Food was grown and also bought from
the local inhabitants, but the pirates needed a market to
dispose of their loot. That market was furnished by the
colonies in America, especially North Carolina and New
York. Captain Samuel Burgess, a relative of the Phillips

family of patroons in New York, and Ort van Tyle were known to have engaged both in piracy and trade with the pirates. Burgess was condemned for his piracy after a trial in London but was pardoned by Queen Anne. Female companionship was a problem for the pirates, and the intercourse with the Malagasy natives led to trouble. Libertatia and other pirate settlements were eventually destroyed by outraged tribesmen. The Madagascar piracy was ended when the powerful British East India Company brought pressure on the British government because the pirates were interfering with the British-Indian trade. Lord Bellamont was sent out to New York as governor to suppress the market for the goods the pirates had taken in the Indian Ocean. He also commissioned Captain Kidd to sail to the Indian Ocean to attack the pirates there. Kidd turned pirate himself, willingly or forced by his crew, and ended as the most famous pirate of them all, although not the most successful.

War had broken out again in Europe, and skilled seamen, both black and white, now could go into a legitimate form of piracy called "privateering." The term was defined by Sir Leoline Jenkins of the British admiralty court in 1670: a "privateer" was a vessel armed and equipped by private individuals which was issued a commission by a sovereign power to "cruise against the enemy." Ships taken by privateers were to be brought into the nearest admiralty court to be examined to determine if they were lawful prizes. If they were adjudged to be "enemy" or carrying enemy goods, they were condemned and sold for the benefit of the captors, minus a commission for the king and the admiralty judge who conducted the examination. Needless to say, few ships were not considered lawful prizes under that profitable system. Privateering had a tremendous advantage over piracy, for captured crewmen of a privateer were considered prisoners of war rather than outlaws subject to hanging from the yardarm. Most of the pirates took advantage of a general pardon issued by George I of England in 1717 to change their status from outlaw-pirates to legitimate privateersmen.

As long as war continued, privateering continued, with crewmen and gunners in short supply. And war did continue: the War of the Spanish Succession, 1701–1713; the war against Spain, 1718; the War of the Austrian Succession, 1740; the Seven Years War, 1756–1763; the American Revolution (which also involved Spain and France against England), 1775–1783; and the French Revolution of 1791, which blended into the Napoleonic Wars and did not end until 1815.

Privateers as well as British naval vessels recognized no color line. Black and white crewmen served together. It is likely that some blacks rose to be officers of privateers. A painting reproduced among the illustrations in this book shows a black privateersman who is either a very rich sailor or an officer, for he carries a sword and telescope and is dressed in an English naval captain's coat. James Forten, later a well-known sailmaker and leader of the black community in Philadelphia, served aboard the privateer *Royal Louis*. Captured by the British, Forten was offered his freedom if he would enlist in the British navy. He preferred to remain an American and was imprisoned on the *Jersey* hulk in New York Harbor for the rest of the war.

Privateering was big business. In the first year of the

War of 1812, seventeen privateers with 1,600 men sailed from Baltimore alone. New York sent out twenty-five privateers with 2,200 men, and the other ports were not far behind, despite a vigorous blockade. Naturally the British also sent out privateers against the American ships. These privateers sailed out of Saint John's, Newfoundland, Halifax, and Jamaica. Ships were often captured and recaptured several times.

There was one special risk for black privateersmen. Any black captured on a privateer in the Caribbean was brought before the admiralty court in Jamaica. There he was considered to be a slave and was sold, as enemy property, back into slavery, despite any evidence that he might be free. Any black captured from an English ship and brought into the French prize court at Martinique was handled the same way. Blacks captured in northern waters or in the English Channel were treated as were whites, and usually ended as prisoners of war in the notorious Dartmoor prison. One of the buildings of that prison, as a matter of fact, was under the unofficial rule of "King" Dick, a black privateersman who ruled effectively over white and black prisoners alike.

Toward the end of the Napoleonic Wars public opinion turned against both privateers and pirates. In 1800 United States warships were in action against privateers and pirates operating out of Haiti and Santo Domingo. The fact that all of these were small sloops or large rowboats manned entirely by blacks made it easier for the American officers to ignore international law. Nobody showed any concern over territorial waters or legal commissions from the governments of Haiti or Santo Domingo, but treated all these privateers as ordinary pirates. The same year American ships also fought against the Barbary pirates of Tripoli.

The Europeans were also getting tired of the pirates. As soon as the British were free of Napoleon in 1816, Lord Exmouth led a combined English-Dutch naval force that blew the pirate stronghold of Algiers into a pile of rubble. The French closed the chapter of North African piracy by occupying Algiers as a "protectorate" in 1830.

In the Caribbean a kind of piracy was to linger on. The upheaval of the revolt of the Spanish colonies released a flood of privateers bearing commissions from the revolutionary governments of what later were to become Mexico, Colombia, Venezuela, and Argentina. Although the American and British governments were friendly to the idea of revolt, the activities of these privateers brought interference by both navies. The smuggling, slave trading, and privateer base of Jean Laffite in Louisiana was broken up in 1816 despite his service in the Battle of New Orleans. An attempt by Laffite to re-establish himself in Galveston (Mexican territory) was also suppressed, despite the fact that he was acting on a commission from the revolutionary government of Mexico. Guns of naval ships overrode the weak legal position of the American naval officers, and Galveston was evacuated and burned.

In 1822 the U.S. Secretary of the Navy authorized Admiral David Porter to land on Cuban soil in pursuit of pirates. Porter reacted with vigor, seizing all likely boats off the coasts of Cuba and Puerto Rico. Since all Cuban fishermen carried knives, it was difficult to distinguish between pirates and fishermen; thus they were all considered pirates without the bother of worrying about evidence.

In one case, for instance, ships from the U.S. West Indian squadron found four houses and eight boats equipped for turtling and fishing. They also discovered a cave with what was claimed to be "plundered goods, none of them very valuable." They confiscated the best of the plunder for their own use and burnt all the rest of the possessions, boats, and houses of the suspect fishermen. Porter was later court-martialed for excessive zeal and conflict with the Cuban civil authorities, but public opinion was with him. Atrocities by pirates were played up in the press, such as the case of the British ship *Blessing*. She was captured off Cuba in 1822 by a "long, black schooner commanded by a white man with a crew of all colors and nations." The captain of the *Blessing* and his son were murdered and the rest of the crew was set adrift. The popular cry for retribution arose regardless of Cuban territoriality.

Captain Canot, later a leading slave trader on the West African coast, served for a time with a group of wrecker-pirates and recounted one incident. His ship from Havana had run aground on shoals off Cuba, where he was hailed by local fishermen who promised to take off the cargo and safeguard it for $1,000. That night the ship was boarded by the same "fishermen" and the crew was hunted down and killed. Canot escaped because one of the pirate chieftains declared he was a "nephew." He then served with the gang. On leaving them he was given two sovereigns by a black member who claimed to have met Canot previously on the docks of Salem, Massachusetts. Canot reported that the loot from these wrecker-pirates was bought by a group of "amphibious jews." After selling their loot, the pirates turned back into being fishermen.

This kind of petty piracy was ended by the joint action

of British and American cruisers and the reluctant cooperation of the Spanish authorities in Cuba. Slave smuggling
was wiped out at the same time by the same means. Privateering was officially outlawed in international law by the
1856 Treaty of Paris.

Watermen

Inshore waters along the American coast provided many blacks with food and a cash crop without a large capital investment. A small boat, often home-built, and some simple equipment made it easy for poor blacks to acquire both a livelihood and the skills that could be usable on larger ships.

The American Indians were the first watermen on the east coast of North America. They used their none-too-seaworthy dugouts and canoes to catch fish and to drag for oysters, mussels, and clams in the bays and estuaries up and down the coast. All of the early European explorers noted the abundance of fish and oysters in their reports. By the end of the 1600's oystering and fishing furnished a steady supply of food for many colonists, both rich and poor.

A French visitor to Virginia in 1687 wrote: "There are so many shell oysters that my host had only to send one of his servants in one of the small boats and two hours after the ebb he brought the boat back full." The servant was, presumably, a black slave.

The great plantation owners along the Virginia rivers were known for their oyster dinners, as were the inns of the capital at Williamsburg. The black slaves had learned quickly to supply this need. At this time oyster tonging was only one of the many waterside activities performed by servants of the "big house." Fishing, oystering, and handling water transportation were often done by the same person. The black fishermen were necessarily allowed a much greater degree of freedom than the field hands. At times the same skill would be used by blacks escaping from slavery, and swamps such as the "Great Dismal" were known hideouts for escaped blacks.

The method of obtaining oysters was simple. Two massive iron rakes were fastened together like a pair of scissors to form twenty-foot-long "oyster tongs," which could be made by any local blacksmith. The tongs were handled by one man operating a small skiff or punt, also locally made. The large plantations had servants designated as "watermen" or "fishermen" to bring in the oysters, but there were so many available that the oyster beds were open to rich and poor alike. Oysters were gathered to eat fresh and some were preserved by drying or pickling. They also served as an export item for trade with the Caribbean islands.

By the early 1800's the oyster banks off New England and New York that had seemed so limitless were becoming exhausted due to overharvesting. Schooners were sent south to the Chesapeake by 1817 to obtain young "seed" oysters to replant the northern beds. The schooners not only brought back "seed" oysters but also southern blacks from the Virginia and Maryland shore to settle in the North.

Soon a chain of black settlements where oystering was the main business stretched from Maryland up along the Jersey coast to Staten Island, New York. One notable settlement was Sandy Ground, a black community in Staten Island founded by black oystermen who primarily came from Snow Hill, Maryland, in 1828.

"Dragging" for oysters also began in the early 1800's in northern bays (it was prohibited on the Chesapeake until after the Civil War). In this operation a heavy iron rake, wider than a "tong," was dragged over the sea bottom and the oysters were raked into a steel mesh net. Dragging can only be done over smooth bottom and requires a larger boat than tonging. Oyster schooners and sloops replaced many of the skiffs, but certain areas remained natural tonging grounds because of the rocky ocean bottom. In the Chesapeake certain additional areas, although suitable for dragging, were specifically reserved for tongers. Most of the black oystermen lacked the capital to buy and equip the larger boats and so remained tongers, selling their catch to "buy-boats" that acted as middlemen. Many white-owned ships signed on black oystermen as crew, but some blacks were able to purchase their own draggers and buy-boats.

The development of railroads and fast packet steamers around the middle of the nineteenth century transformed the oyster business. Demand for oysters shot up tremendously, for they could now be shipped beyond the shore points without spoiling. The coming of refrigerator cars simply accelerated this trend. There were two thousand "dragging" schooners and over six thousand tongers at work on the Chesapeake alone around 1880.

No longer did the oysterman sell most of his catch directly to consumers. Instead it went to a packing house, possibly by way of a buy-boat. There the oysters were "shucked"—opened and cut loose from the shell—then packed on ice and shipped fresh. Many black women as well as men went to work in these oyster houses as "shuckers," being paid on a piecework basis. The packers were summoned by the whistle of the packing house as soon as the oyster boats were sighted coming in. It was a feast-or-famine business.

Oyster packers and wholesale dealers, in order to ensure their regular supply, began to lease parts of the ocean bottom from state and local governments. These areas favorable to oyster growth became "leaseholds," which were "farmed" by seeding them with young oysters in spring and dragging up full-grown oysters in fall and winter. Oystermen working the licensed beds often became employees or sharecroppers of the packer-entrepreneur. Poachers working on leased beds were driven off by rifle-armed guards. On the other hand, some draggers had no hesitation about raiding oyster beds supposedly reserved for tongers, many of them black. In the 1880's many draggers were captained by men who "feared neither man, God or the devil" and crewed by Irish and German immigrants picked up by crimps working the Baltimore dock areas. On a number of recorded occasions these "hard-cases" rammed and sank tongers in the Chesapeake who were working their traditional beds. The black tongers had little recourse: a black who shot a white was severely punished no matter what the provocation. The open aggression of the draggers did not cease until Virginia and Maryland equipped an "oyster-navy" with enough artillery to enforce the law on the spot.

Staten Island whites were especially active in leasing oyster beds. Starting with the oyster grounds in the Raritan Bay off New York Harbor, they expanded their holdings to Long Island Sound, the Jersey coast, and finally the Delaware and Chesapeake Bays. The blacks of Sandy Ground and other communities became employees and contractors. The fact that so much of the oyster grounds was owned by one group helped expand the drift of blacks northward, for the same kind of boats and the same employers could be found along the entire middle Atlantic coast.

Blacks, however, were never entirely driven out of the independent oyster business. Many blacks owned restaurants and worked as caterers or cooks in the fine hotels and aboard passenger steamers, and they probably preferred dealing with their fellow blacks. This ensured a protected market for the black oystermen. South of New York there were always a number of black oystermen, but north of that state line the oyster boats were dominated by Yankees, Irish, and Italians.

Today, pollution has destroyed the oyster beds in New York Harbor and on most of Delaware Bay; all oystering was banned on Chesapeake Bay in 1976 because of chemical pollution. The fate of the black oysterman and his white counterpart is now in jeopardy.

Oysters were and are only one of the plentiful products of the Atlantic shore—and a seasonal one at that. In the summer when oysters are not fit for eating, the blue crab becomes readily available. Like the oyster, the crabs are found in relatively shallow water and can be caught from small boats with simple equipment.

Crabs in migration can be "dipped up" in a simple net. But the more common method is by setting a "trot-line," a number of short pieces of string hung at intervals from a long line. The short pieces are baited with chicken necks or dead fish, and the whole line is laid in the water with a marker at each end. Starting from one end, the crabber pulls up the string. Crabs hold on to the bait while the string is being pulled up and can be netted before they drop off. Like oystering, however, the work is neither easy nor without danger. Many an oysterman or crabber has fallen out of the boat while reaching over the side for his catch, or has drowned when a sudden storm overturned his loaded boat. Working usually alone, he is only missed when his boat fails to return at night. The major crabbing territory coincides with the major distribution of black watermen: from Staten Island to the Georgia coast.

At the beginning, crabbing, like oystering, was only a subsistence activity. After the Civil War this changed to a large extent, although many a waterman and boy still got his crabs "for the pot." In 1866 the railway penetrated to Crisfield, Maryland, and a large crab industry developed. Crab traps and larger boats replaced the less efficient trot-line, and crabs were rushed to the big cities packed on ice. Deviled crab on the half shell became so popular that packers included one hundred empty shells with each gallon of "picked" (removed from the shell) meat. Little Negro boys, called "knockers," were employed to clean and dry these shells. Black women, working at piecework rates, picked the meat from the crabs. Most of the crab meat was shipped on ice, but packing houses in Hampton, Virginia, started canning crabs as early as 1874. The crab picking houses encouraged nearby settlements of black workers by renting them quarters close to the factory, although often at high rents. At the same time the men of these settlements "share-cropped" in company-owned boats, trot-lining in summer and tonging for oysters in winter.

Many of the crab boats on the Chesapeake today use sophisticated steel traps. The boats are captained by decendants of the original white settlers of Smith and Tangier islands. These islanders considered anything that floated, swam, and crawled in their marshes as their exclusive property. The attitude still persists, and although theoretically anyone can take out a crabbing license, a stranger putting down traps or lines is apt to find them gone the next day. Thus Chesapeake blacks traditionally trot-line their crabs instead of trapping. Farther south, along the Carolina Sounds where there is not the same strong feeling of "ownership" as among the Maryland islanders, more blacks have found their way into commercial crabbing.

In the West Indies there are neither blue crabs nor oysters, but the conch shell is exploited in the same way by one-man boats. Catching the spiny lobster off the Bahamas, banks is a more recent industry carried out as a commercial venture by larger boats.

Shrimping on the Carolina and Georgia coasts was started by white men relying on European experience. By 1800, however, the crews of the Atlantic shrimping boats were mostly blacks, although owners and captains were whites, at least until recently. Crews were hired by the "shape-up" system: captains would pick their crews from the men standing on the docks. This pattern was found at Wilmington, North Carolina, and other ports along the coast. Payment for crew members was both cash and part of the catch. Shrimp was brought home, cooked, then peddled in small quantities in the black community by both children and adults. Shrimping on the Gulf of Mexico, on the other hand, is the domain of the French-speaking Acadians, and few or no blacks are found on shrimping boats there.

Despite many handicaps facing black watermen who wish to operate in a cash economy, the marshes and shallow waters offer many opportunities for subsistence activities. The relatively free life has attracted blacks to the shores for years, even before the end of slavery. On the Sea Islands off the coast of Georgia and South Carolina, African customs and language patterns are better preserved than anywhere else in the United States.

Blacks had another advantage over whites in the coastal areas. The African genetic heritage made many Africans fever-proof. The sickle cell trait renders many of them immune from malaria, and they also have genetic resistance to the dreaded yellow fever. Until recently, few white men remained healthy in these mosquito-ridden areas. This circumstance reduced visits by slave catchers, overseers, tax collectors, and other representatives of white authority.

One way swamp and island blacks obtained necessary protein to supplement the corn from farms was by what the inhabitants of the eastern shore of Maryland call "progging." This includes any and all products obtained by poking around marsh holes. Turtles were caught by "hollering": the hunter would make a loud noise, which caused the turtle to stick its head up. The hunter then circled behind the turtle and grabbed it by the back of its

Cast-net fishing in African lagoons. Similar nets are used by Gullah-speaking blacks of the Carolina and Georgia coasts in the United States. FAO PHOTO BY G. TORTOLI

Fishermen on the West African coast had to become superb boat-men to survive the wave and current conditions. This picture shows a swamped fishing boat on the coast of Dahomey. FAO PHOTO BY A. DEFEVER

An Egyptian sailing a boat on the Nile today. The Nubians of Egypt are believed to have voyaged to America before the birth of Christ. AMERICAN MUSEUM OF NATURAL HISTORY

Native Swahili dhows in the harbor of Zanzibar. They were sailed along the East African coast and to India for centuries before arrival of the Portuguese. THE PEABODY MUSEUM OF SALEM

Slave traffic on the coast of Africa. Eighteenth-century engraving.
CHICAGO HISTORICAL SOCIETY

Painting of the *Amistad* depicting the freed slaves going ashore to
seek food and a navigator to take them back to Africa. NEW HAVEN
COLONY HISTORICAL SOCIETY

Portrait of "Cinque" at the time of his trial, painted by Nathaniel Jocelyn. NEW HAVEN HISTORICAL SOCIETY.

Below: Slave cargo at sea. MELTZER COLLECTION OF THE SCHOMBURG COLLECTION, NEW YORK PUBLIC LIBRARY

Black privateersman during the Revolutionary War. Newport, Rhode Island, c. 1780. This recently discovered painting is privately owned. PHOTO COURTESY OF NEWPORT BICENTENNIAL COMMISSION

Below: Crew list of a suspected slaver bound for Cuba from the Cape Verde Islands. NATIONAL ARCHIVES, CONSULAR LETTERS, SANTIAGO

Stokers on a riverboat. Blacks made up more than half of the crews employed on Mississippi steamboats. MELTZER COLLECTION OF THE SCHOMBURG COLLECTION, NEW YORK PUBLIC LIBRARY

Crew of the Chesapeake steamer *Middlesex* unloading cargo at Lodge Landing, Virginia. Seamen frequently had to double as longshoremen on coastal ships. MARINERS MUSEUM

Black oysterman tonging oysters from a "Yankee skiff." Picture taken off Staten Island, New York, c. 1906. PHOTO COURTESY STATEN ISLAND INSTITUTE OF ARTS & SCIENCES

Cooper sealing turpentine barrels on Savannah docks (from a stereopticon slide). MICHAEL COHN COLLECTION

Stepping the mast on the schooner *Skyway*, Bequia
St. Vincent, West Indies. DOUGLAS C. PYLE

Half-model of the schooner *Alexis* built by Canute Calliste on
Carriacou Island, Grenada, in the 1950's. H. D. HARTMAN

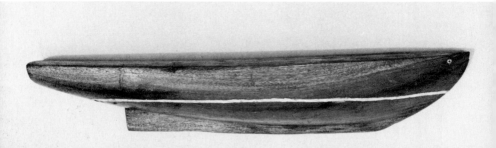

As the four-masted schooner *Doris Hamlin,* heeling before a strong northwester, sails down Chesapeake Bay from Baltimore to Newport News, Virginia, to load coal for Bermuda, able-bodied seaman Albert Scott steers, lower right. At far left is the schooner's master, Captain George H. Hopkins, with Mrs. Hopkins seated. October, 1936. ROBERT H. BURGESS

Logwood piled on the main deck of the four-masted schooner *Doris Hamlin* of Baltimore, being loaded for Baltimore at Cap Haitien, Haiti, December, 1936. ROBERT H. BURGESS

Above: "Black Charley" (Hoyt), seated, the last shipping master for sailing craft in New York City. Standing is Edward Jordan, a distant cousin and steward of the four-masted schooner *Annie C. Ross.* Aboard the *Ross* about 1939. JOHN A. NOBLE

Left: Fireman on the tug *Peerless,* out of Norfolk, Virginia. THE MARINERS MUSEUM

Caulking a deck seam. M. V. BREWINGTON

Half of the crew of the four-masted schooner *Elizabeth Bandi*, built in Gulfport, Mississippi, in 1919, was black. "NO" on the life ring indicates home port New Orleans. The schooner survives as the restaurant ship *Seute Deern* in Hamburg, Germany. SOUTH STREET SEAPORT LIBRARY

Young whaling crew mincing blubber aboard the bark *California*. Cape Verdeans were often recruited at the age of twelve. THE PEABODY MUSEUM OF SALEM

Below: Bringing a "try-out" kettle aboard a small whaler about 1905. COLLECTION OF H. HARRISON HUSTER

Menhaden men tightening a net. H. DAVID HARTMAN

Mullet fishermen. U.S. COMMISSION OF FISHERIES

The *Ernestina,* last of the Cape Verde packets, on her way to Operation Sail '76. She was the only African participant with an all-Cape Verdean crew. The next day she was dismasted in the Atlantic. ALBERTO LOPES

Sailmakers at work aboard a New Bedford whaling ship. WHALING MUSEUM, NEW BEDFORD, MASSACHUSETTS

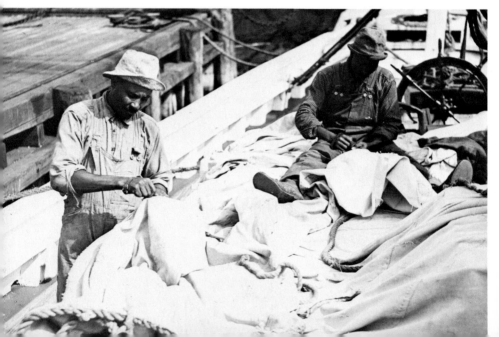

Above: Seaman Joao Gomes, originally of the Cape Verde Islands, sailed the *Ernestina* to the United States in 1949. MIRIAM MARCY

Right: Captain Pedro Evora, last skipper of the *Ernestina,* navigated to the United States in 1965, without benefit of radar or other sophisticated gear. T. STEPHEN TEGU

Civil War transport *Wauhatchie*.

Captain and crew of the Liberty ship *Frederick Douglass*. John Clarke of New York, third mate; Vincent Davis, chief engineer; Charles Harris of Pawtucket, Rhode Island, assistant engineer; Captain Adrian Richardson of Dutch West Indies; Ferdinand Smith, Secretary of National Maritime Union. SCHOMBURG COLLECTION, NEW YORK PUBLIC LIBRARY

shell. Both diamondback turtles and snapping turtles fell victim to black hunters using this simple method. In addition, eels and other fish could be speared in the shallow waters of the estuaries.

Swampland from Massachusetts to Georgia furnished a crop that could be harvested only by watermen. Salt hay is less nutritious than land-grown grasses but makes excellent bedding for cattle and horses. It also makes a cheap and effective compost. Rushes for basket weaving also came from the swamps, and black basket weavers were known all along the coast. In some cases the black basket weavers used European or American Indian patterns, but in others the baskets were similiar to those made in Senegal on the west coast of Africa.

Many of the watermen also set "pounds," large fish traps. Pounds are especially effective in catching migrating fish. When the drumfish were running off the Sea Islands, for instance, even the family ox could expect some time off from plowing.

The marshes, estuaries, and shallow waters were a resource that could be and was exploited by the blacks living nearby. There competition and regulation was at its lowest, and life was free, if difficult.

VI

Shipbuilders

The day of the launching of a schooner on the island of Carriacou in the West Indies is a "Big Time." Between five hundred and a thousand people may gather for the fete. The women begin preparing food and the men butcher animals at dawn. By ten o'clock in the morning some men are sharpening axes to be used in "cutting down" the hull of the ship from its timber supports. On deck, the priest prays for the safety and success of the vessel while a band plays and people sing. The flag is unfurled and for the first time the general public learns the ship's name, which has been sewn into the flag. The priest then leaves the deck and the axe men begin to cut her down; each man cuts at the supporting logs in turn until the vessel is lying on its starboard side on the rollers. By early afternoon the schooner is launched by hauling it into the sea to the accompaniment of sea chanties. Once the ship is floating and has righted itself, the captain jumps into the water and breaks bottles of champagne over the stern. Boys climb aboard and begin rocking her back and forth. The fete continues far into the night. Food and drink provided for one "Big Time" launching included twenty cases of rum, six cases of whiskey, one case of champagne, twenty cases of soft drinks, a bull weighing over five hundred pounds, two large pigs, seventy sheep and goats, seventy-five chickens, twenty bunches of bananas, two bags of rice, and two bags of sweet potatoes. Launching a ship is truly a festive occasion for the entire community. In one way or another, the coastal communities feel a strong tie to the new craft, to the men who built her, and to those who are to sail her.

The day before the launching has been a "helping day" when many men come to donate their labor. They set rough logs as supports along the side of the vessel and lay planks parallel to the beam of the ship for it to lie on at launching. In the afternoon they finish the final coat of paint, clean up the ship, and nail the bilge boards in place.

The process of shipbuilding starts with conversations between the owner and the master shipwright. The owner describes exactly what he has in mind. He talks about the size of the vessel, carrying capacity, and expected speed balanced against safety and cost factors. Then the shipwright builds a small model of the proposed boat. Building ship models is a common practice among the boys of the island, but it reaches artistic dimensions in the hands of a skilled shipwright. The model is then shown to the owner, who approves the design or requests changes based on his experience or prejudices. Once the model reflects the intentions of the owner, lumber is assembled and "setting up" of the schooner begins.

Setting up the frame of a boat on Carriacou is also a

big occasion. Shipwrights and others are invited. They freely give their assistance and work hard to complete the setting up by day's end. The keel is laid down. To it are bolted the stem, center frame, bow frame, and stern post. Long strips of board, called ribbons, are then nailed to these frames to show the shape of the boat and to keep the frames firm. As the frames are set, logs are placed in the ground to brace the vessel as it is being built. Planking the sides is next, and then the deck has to be laid.

The next step is "caulking" with oakum, a mixture of pitch and frayed hemp from old rope used to seal the seams of the ship. The oakum is rolled into long rolls that are carried twisted around the arms of the caulker. He pounds this mixture into the seams with a caulking iron and mallet. After the oakum is "tufted" into the seam, the wheel is applied to it and the oakum rolled down until it will set no deeper. This is a skilled job, opening seams that are too tight and stuffing the looser ones, which allows the planks to "give" without the boat leaking. Caulking makes a ship flexible when the waves hit it, instead of rigid and brittle, and is one of the big advantages of a wooden hull. Any excess pitch is then scraped off and the planks are cleaned and sanded before painting begins. After several coats of paint, the ship is ready for launching.

Work continues for weeks or months after launching. Carpenters build the cabin, sailmakers cut a "suit" of sails, spars and masts are rounded, and then the masts are set into the keel. The ship is then rigged with ropes for handling the sails and is ready for loading for its maiden voyage.

On the island of Carriacou blacks have been building

ships since at least 1833. Many of the vessels were small sloops or schooners under fifty tons, but despite their small size they were capable of voyages anywhere. Some are used for trade with neighboring islands but others are sold off-island. The details of launching might differ in other small shipbuilding centers in American waters, but methods of construction do not change much for wooden ships.

The building of "Jamaica sloops" was one of the earliest forms of shipbuilding on this side of the Atlantic Ocean. These sloops were popular in the West Indies and elsewhere before 1725. They were used for piracy and for the intermittent warfare of the period as well as for trading. They were small, handy, shallow-draft vessels carrying large sails on a raking mast. The bowsprits were enormous, and their fore-and-aft sails were often supplemented by a square topsail. Cargo-carrying capacity, safety, and comfort were sacrificed to handiness, speed, and a wide deck on which to mount guns. Weapons were necessary because trade of the period meant smuggling since colonial nations, Spanish, French, and English tried to prevent the Americans and islanders from trading with anyone except the mother country. "Jamaica-type" sloops soon were being built over a wide area, and their construction spread to Bermuda.

Bermuda became the leading shipbuilding community in American waters because of the availability of good quality cedar wood, which was rot resistant while being light and strong. Soon the Jamaica sloops became known as "Bermuda sloops." There was constant contact between Bermuda and Virginia, the same families having settled in both places. Shipbuilding ideas traveled with the family

visitors. By 1800 the Bermuda sloops had evolved into
the famous "Baltimore Clippers," low-lying two-masted
schooners rather than single-masted sloops, still carrying
the large sail area on raking masts. They could carry a
large crew and heavy guns, but their shallow hulls limited
their cargo-carrying capacity. According to one author,
these schooners were "sired by war, mothered by privateering and piracy and nursed by the cruelty of the slave
trade." They were ideal for privateers in the West Indies,
opium smugglers in China, and slavers in Africa. Later
they were also used for the fruit trade, where speed was
essential. The designers of the Jamaica sloops and their
successors are unknown, but it seems likely that this radical
departure from European prototypes involved the black
population as designers as well as builders. By 1800 almost
all of the shipwrights in the islands were blacks. In the
Chesapeake Bay area of the mainland almost all of the
caulkers and many of the ship carpenters were also blacks.

European and New England schooners of the eighteenth
and nineteenth centuries were different. They were
heavier, with higher decks and slightly less speed but better
sea-keeping ability, necessary in the cold northern seas.
Naturally both groups adapted each other's ideas to some
extent, but the basic ship types remained distinct. White
shipbuilders in some northern yards copied Bermuda and
Baltimore designs whenever the particular qualities of
speed and wide decks were needed. The French also built
some adaptations of the "Jamaica" or "Baltimore" types as
privateers. The British navy, although mainly using ships
of the northern type, commissioned a whole class of Bermuda cutters in 1804. They were fast and handy but never

comfortable riding. No matter if the "Bermuda" ships were cutter rigged or sloops or schooners—they were so fast that they sometimes were "sailed under" the waves and swamped.

Although some ships continued to be built on any convenient beach by owner, master shipwright, and volunteer labor, regular commercial shipyards with hired professionals were set up in Baltimore, New York, and Maine. There, as in naval shipyards, the general artisan who could "turn his hand to anything" was replaced by workers doing one job only. Free and slave labor, white and black, adapted to the new system.

Frederick Douglass, later known as a revolutionary leader and abolitionist, worked as a slave-caulker in a shipyard in East Baltimore. His associates were free blacks, and the prevailing wage in 1839 was $1.50 a day. As a slave Douglass had to turn over most of his wages to his owner. To escape from slavery, Douglass fled north with the help of a white sailor. In New York he found that the waterfront was haunted by slave-catchers and kidnappers and that southern black shipbuilders were definitely unwelcome. Farther north, in New Bedford, Massachusetts, Douglass found that he was only permitted to do unskilled work in the shipyard, regardless of his qualifications. His co-workers told him in no uncertain terms that if he were allowed to do skilled work such as caulking, every white worker in the yard would lay down his tools and walk off the job. Because of this prejudice Douglass worked at cutting wood for whaling ship stoves, loaded ships as a common laborer, and worked in a foundry making brass fittings for ships. Like many another black after him, Douglass found that skin color was a definite factor in what trade a man was allowed to follow in New York and New England. Free was not always equal, even in the relatively open society of the waterfront. In the southern states, as long as skin color determined social status regardless of the job held, blacks were freer to enter occupations. In many of the northern states social status depended on the job held, so blacks were kept out of higher ranking jobs.

Three years after escaping from slavery Douglass told of his life at a meeting of the Massachusetts Anti-Slavery Society in Nantucket. His speech impressed the leaders of the abolitionists and they hired him as a propagandist for the society. He remained a sought-after speaker, thinker, and revolutionary leader until his death in 1895.

James Forten was another black abolitionist who made his living on the waterfront. As a fifteen-year-old, Forten had shipped out on a privateer and had been captured by the British. Profiting by his seagoing experience, Forten set up a sailmaking loft in Philadelphia, which had the largest black population of any city in the United States. He employed twenty-five workers in his sail loft, both blacks and whites. In 1817 he was well enough known to become president of the Anti-Colonization Society, which opposed sending all blacks to Africa or Haiti as proposed by Captain Cuffee and others. When he died in 1819, Forten left an estate valued at over $100,000.

South of Philadelphia this pattern of black caulkers, carpenters, coopers, and rope makers persisted. But north of that line blacks were only allowed to function in these trades when servicing small fishing and coastal ships outside of the industrialized shipyards.

In the industrialized North, job opportunities attracted

immigrants from all over. In the years 1848 and 1849, events in Europe were to have a decisive effect on the role of blacks in shipbuilding. A series of unsuccessful popular uprisings in France, Germany, Austria, and Hungary brought skilled European artisans to America to compete with the blacks as carpenters, painters, and iron workers. At the same time the disastrous potato crop failure in Ireland brought thousands of starving and desperate Irishmen to compete for the unskilled jobs as laborers on the American waterfront. Irish longshoremen could even be found working on the docks of Mississippi River ports. Competition for jobs might be fought out with physical force, and in that case, the Irish could count on help from their fellow Irishmen on the police forces of the cities. In addition, the fugitive slave laws had been strengthened in an effort to avert the Civil War. The more extreme elements in the North formed the "American" or "Know-Nothing" Party. Its platform was anti-Catholic, anti-black, anti-Irish, and anti-immigrant, and it elected some thirty-four congressmen with those slogans. Since movement to other jobs was often blocked on social and religious grounds, job competition between black and Irish on the docks remained strong. The conflict became stronger during the Civil War when newly freed blacks drifted north. Since the draft took whites but not blacks, white resentment and fear about loss of jobs resulted in race riots. The worst trouble came during the "Draft Riots" in New York in 1863: white mobs stormed and burned police stations and the Negro orphan asylum, lynched blacks, and committed other outrages. It took the Army three days to restore order.

Attitudes did not improve after the war. Jobs were

scarce and employers used blacks to depress wages. When the caulkers of Boston struck for an eight-hour day in 1867, shipyard owners brought black caulkers from Portsmouth, Virginia, to break the strike. The memory of these and other black-white conflicts resulted in the early craft unions wanting to have nothing to do with either individual black craftsmen as members or even black locals. As unions became stronger, this feeling operated to drive the blacks away from the skilled shipbuilding jobs which they had held. In most cases this pressure also prevented training blacks for the newly created trades such as welding and riveting, which were introduced with the coming of steel-hulled ships in the 1880's.

Where the small wooden ship remained a way of life and industrialization did not take hold, black artisans remained, continuing to build ships in the tradition of the "Jamaica sloop" and the "Baltimore clipper." In the Bahamas, Puerto Rico, Barbados, and Carriacou, some of the old shipbuilding skills can still be found among the blacks. These skills and the availability of good wood have brought a recent revival of wooden yacht building and repair at Belize and Bequia in the Caribbean.

When the blacks were driven out of the shipyards in the United States, Homer Ferguson, the paternalistic owner of the Newport News Shipbuilding Company, decided to follow a different policy. In his yards there were up to twenty-three hundred blacks employed at unskilled and skilled jobs. There was no union at Newport News, and ships were produced cheaper than anywhere else. When this company expanded to Wilmington, North Carolina, the same policy was followed.

World War I brought thirty thousand blacks into the shipbuilding industry. However, they were not able to obtain membership in the boilermaker and machinist unions that controlled the yards and so were confined to unskilled jobs. After the war the unorganized blacks were the first men to be fired, again except in the yards of the Newport News Shipbuilding Company.

During the emergency of World War II blacks once more entered the shipbuilding yards. At the Kaiser shipyards in California, six thousand blacks worked as shipwrights, stage riggers, shipfitters, joiners, boilermakers, and painters as well as unskilled laborers. At the Bethlehem yards in Baltimore, seventy-five hundred black workers were employed; the work force at the North Carolina Shipbuilding Company was 30 percent black.

The role of the Negro was recognized by the government in naming thirteen liberty ships after prominent black Americans: the *Booker T. Washington, George Washington Carver, Frederick Douglass, John Merrick, Robert L. Vann, Paul Laurence Dunbar, James Weldon Johnson, John Hope, John H. Murphy, Robert S. Abbott, Edward Savoy, Toussaint L'Ouverture,* and *Harriet Tubman.* The destroyer escort U.S.S. *Harmon* was named after a black messman who lost his life in the Battle of Guadalcanal.

Because of government insistence under various legislative acts, blacks are assuming a larger role in the U.S. shipbuilding industry, and increased training of Blacks is carried on under the affirmative action programs.

VII

Deepwater Seamen

When Paul Cuffee died in 1817 he left an estate of twenty thousand dollars—a sizable fortune for a black man in the nineteenth century. He owned a fleet of ships and employed hundreds of white and black sailors. He had started thirty-eight years before with only a small open boat, which he used to transport farm goods and fish from Cuttyhunk to New Bedford. His first boat was seized by white men, but he built another large enough to sail to Nantucket and back. There was a need for small boats to link the smaller communities, and he prospered. He also started a fish-packing business in Westport, his home, and took his boat as far north as Newfoundland to pick up codfish to be salted and packed in Westport for shipment to other communities. Paul Cuffee had two boats and a crew of eight when he decided to undertake his first whaling expedition. He had gone whaling as a boy and his brothers-in-law were whalers, but this would be the first time a whaling ship would be captained by a black. His ships were too small and ill-equipped, so he had to

persuade the captain of another whaling ship to help
process the larger whales they caught. But his men proved
capable, and they brought in six whales. The blubber was
boiled down to oil, and Cuffee sold it in Philadelphia for
a good profit.

With this money he built a sixty-nine-ton schooner,
which he named the *Ranger*. The leading merchant of
New Bedford, William Rotch, became his patron and
gave him steady shipping contracts. On his first voyage he
took the *Ranger* to Norfolk, Virginia, to pick up corn. He
then sailed regularly between Philadelphia and New Bedford. He was growing rich and he built another ship, a
two-masted square rigger he called the *Traveller*.

Paul Cuffee had long been interested in improving the
condition of Negroes in America. He had been instrumental in obtaining the right to vote for free Negroes in
Massachusetts by petitioning the legislature and refusing
to pay his taxes. He established one of the first interracial
schools in the United States. Despite his success, he suffered daily discrimination and thought emigration back
to Africa would be a solution for the Negroes in the
United States.

On January 1, 1811, he sailed with the *Traveller* for
Sierra Leone, the English colony of free blacks founded
in 1787, to acquaint himself with the condition of the
colony. He discussed the needs of the colony with the governor and the black leaders, secured from them authority
to bring over skilled Negroes from the United States, and
proposed the organization of the "Friendly Society of
Sierra Leone" to promote the general improvement of the
colony. The black sea captain and his all-black crew plus

three apprentices from Sierra Leone sailed to London, where they were hailed as a credit to their race and were encouraged in the project by British leaders of the anti-slavery movement. Cuffee then returned to America to look for suitable persons to send back. However, the War of 1812 intervened, and it was not until 1815 that he was able to sail with nine families and thirty-eight persons for Sierra Leone. He personally paid most of the costs of the voyage; moreover, he was unable to sell any of the goods he had bought to trade due to British trade prohibitions.

When he returned, his efforts were attacked by James Forten, the prominent black Philadelphia sailmaker and his good friend, for playing into the hands of the Southern racists who were also encouraging the emigration of all free blacks. Paul Cuffee gave up any further plans for colonizing Sierra Leone. He became ill and died on September, 9, 1817. He had given American blacks a vision of a free, productive African society, and by his own personal example he had shown that Negroes could captain and manage a large commercial fleet as well as any white man if given the opportunity.

In the early nineteenth century Negroes were active at all levels in the maritime industry as pilots, shipwrights, deckhands, and stevedores. The American merchant fleet was expanding rapidly, and a man was hired for his abilities, not the color of his skin. Experienced sailors were so valued that Massachusetts appointed agents at Charleston and New Orleans to look after the rights of Negro seamen aboard her ships. Forty percent of the free Negroes in Boston are believed to have been involved with the maritime industry in 1830. In New York a colored sailor's boardinghouse was established in 1839 to provide for the needs of approximately three thousand Negro seamen who sailed out of New York each year. It has been estimated that in 1850 half of the American seamen were black.

Negro mariners who had made the sea their profession were obviously preferable to young white boys or undependable alcoholics who had failed at other careers on land. A young white man would ship out to gain experience or save a little money to start another career, but for most blacks there was no other alternative but to ship out again.

Even when white sailors were available, Negroes were often preferred for they were more easily controlled and often could be paid less. Captain McGowan of the *Benvenue* hired all Negroes for the port watch to balance the Irishmen he hired for the starboard watch. There was extreme competition between the two watches. The Negroes were from Carroll County, Virginia, where seagoing had been a tradition for centuries, and they were all experienced Cape Horners. The Irishmen deeply resented the privileges given the blacks. After a few inconclusive fights, the two groups were determined to best each other by driving the ship faster during their watch. The shrewd Scot captain thereby obtained the best possible results by fomenting racial rivalry. Usually, however, a man's abilities were quickly recognized, and a natural grouping developed among the sailors.

A sailor's lot aboard the merchantmen of the nineteenth century was not enviable. They were almost completely at the mercy of the captain. During a storm or when trying to round Cape Horn, men were knocked senseless by waves crashing over the deck and many suffered broken arms, legs, or ribs as they were smashed against the railing or deckhouse if they were lucky—otherwise they were swept overboard. Most sailors sported scars on their skulls, shins, kneecaps, and hands. Many contracted diseases that were never properly treated. Sailors frequently complained of starvation to their consuls when they finally reached port. They were never paid enough so they could start another life ashore, but were usually in debt to the ship company. Their only solace was alcohol and perhaps a prostitute. In most ports there were special bars for the Negro seamen. In New York, for example, there was the Black and Tan Concert Hall on South Street for men of color. When they ran out of money, crimps would pick them up in the seedy hotels and bars near the harbors and drop them drunk aboard departing ships.

Men often shipped out together in gangs. Frequently blacks would recruit other blacks. The last shipping master to collect men in New York for sailing ships was a black man, Charlie Hoyt. "Black Charlie" had been a mate of the *Albert Willis* and had shipped out men for twenty years in New York Harbor.

By 1870 there were 8,500 Negro seamen shipping out of New York. In 1876 Harry Dean, great-grandson of Paul Cuffee, sailed at age twelve from New York around the world with his uncle and a half black crew aboard the *Traveller*. It took them three weeks to beat around Cape Horn, but they finally made California where another Cuffee was a shipping merchant; they then stopped in Peru, Hawaii, China, India, Zanzibar, Mozambique, Cape Town, Saint Helena, Liberia, Morocco, Italy, Egypt, and

England. Life aboard the deepwater merchant ships was harsh, but it exposed the black sailors to new worlds. Captain Dean was later to establish a shipping company based in Africa, and he even attempted to found a free African state. William Leidesdorff, originally from the Virgin Islands, ran a profitable shipping business between San Francisco and Hawaii and became one of the city's leading traders.

With the arrival of the German, Scandinavian, and Irish immigrants who were willing to work for starvation wages, blacks were slowly being displaced on the merchant ships. In 1890 only 30 percent of the seamen on American ships were U.S. citizens. Shipowners hired large numbers of Orientals and Europeans to prevent unionization of the seamen. As steamships replaced sailing vessels, the companies held that no special skills were required and any common laborer would do.

James Williams, a red-haired Negro from New Bedford, was instrumental in the organization of the Atlantic Coast Seamen's Union and the strike of the Winter of 1893–94 which laid up 50 percent of the deep sea tonnage. He and his friends would waylay non-union men who were willing to ship out for eighteen dollars a month (the union was demanding thirty dollars) and "there were many broken heads before we were through." He was made business agent in New York, and by 1900 ninety five percent of the coasting sailors were union members. Williams and other blacks helped form the Marine Firemen's Union and made up 25 percent of its membership. The Marine Cooks and Stewards Association created a branch office exclusively for blacks. For most of the next fifty years, blacks were kept below decks and were restricted to cook and steward positions.

World War I brought back into commission practically all the old sailing vessels, among them more than one hundred schooners. They were sent mainly to the French port of Brest, carrying bulk cargo for the American Expeditionary Force. The crew for these transport vessels were Negroes recruited mainly in the West Indies.

During 1918 Henry Howard, head of the U.S. Shipping Board Recruiting Service, was told that the large supply of black labor in the South could be useful in manning the ships required for the war. Howard, a former Boston business executive, felt it was "not practicable" to train blacks in ships based in northern ports but he was willing to have them train as firemen in a segregated ship established for that purpose in the South. Accordingly, in August 1918 the steamer *Manderville* was chartered from the Louisiana Steamboat and Ferry Company for one year. When the war ended and there was no longer the great need for seamen, her career as a training ship for blacks was ended.

Until World War II, finding jobs aboard oceangoing ships was extremely difficult for blacks. Hugh Mulzac, the first black man to obtain his Masters license in the United States and who served on over twenty ships, was again a paperhanger in 1920. Marcus Garvey, the charismatic leader of the Universal Negro Improvement Association, was organizing a black-owned and operated steamship company and asked Mulzac to skipper the first ship, the S.S. *Frederick Douglass.* Mulzac put the old *Yarmouth* back into shape and sailed her to triumphant receptions in Cuba, Jamaica, Panama, Philadelphia, and New York. Unfortunately, the Black Star Line was badly run, and after two profitless trips to the Caribbean the *Yarmouth* was laid up at Staten Island. Mulzac had started a Nautical Academy to teach navigation, engineering, and wireless to young blacks; it also collapsed when the Black Star Line was declared bankrupt and there appeared to be no possibilities for blacks aboard ships. Mulzac himself was again unemployed and had to take a job as a steward.

The 1920's and 1930's were hard for seamen, black and white. As an army of unemployed seamen swarmed around every dock looking for work, wages fell from $65 a month, paid able-bodied seamen under the World War I Shipping Board agreement, to as low as $25—seven cents an hour. The International Seamen's Union, which had fought for the Seamen's Act of 1915 guaranteeing seamen basic rights and living conditions, called a strike when it became apparent all was being taken away. The shipowners responded with a lockout and set up special employment halls where strikebreakers could come in under police protection. The companies again hired non-Americans— only 35 percent of the crews were native American in the 1920's—and broke the union.

Hugh Mulzac and other black seamen joined the fledgling Marine Workers Industrial Union because it succeeded in establishing a central hiring hall in Baltimore and took a strong position against racial discrimination (in a two-month period they struck fifty ships to enforce democratic hiring procedures). The ISU and the MWIU were about equal in strength, but neither could obtain recognition from shipowners. The ISU leadership, fearing the growing strength of the more radical MWIU, signed a "quickie" agreement with the shipowners providing for no wage increases, no overtime, and no union hiring hall. There was immediate resentment among the rank and file of the ISU over the "sellout," and all MWIU members were urged to join the ISU to get rid of the corrupt leadership of the ISU. The rank and file elected a Seamen's Defense Committee to push their demands. They published their own newspaper, had gained 20,000 supporters by the fall of 1936, and voted to join the striking West Coast longshoremen against the orders of the ISU leadership. The companies hired goons to beat up the striking seamen, and looked for scabs among the blacks. Hugh Mulzac was offered the job of captain by the Calmar Line, which had denied him a position for twelve years. However, he, like thousands of blacks, joined the strike, although the ISU then only admitted blacks into the Marine Cooks and Stewards Union. After the shipowners capitulated, a new union was formed. The National Maritime Union abolished the autonomous deck, engine, and steward's divisions and provided in its constitution that "there shall be no discrimination because of race, color, political creed, religion or national origin." The national secretary of the NMU was a Negro, Ferdinand Smith. The NMU steadfastly protected the rights of Negro seamen to be hired on a "first in, first out" basis, even in Southern cities, and forced the president of the United States to issue a statement that "questions of race, creed, and color have no place in determining who are to man our ships."

As World War II started and America required the full participation of her Negro seamen, President Roosevelt set aside several Liberty Ships for Negroes to crew. After

twenty-four years as a steward, Captain Mulzac was invited
to command the *Booker T. Washington,* but he refused
to sail with an all-black crew. He was finally allowed to
choose his own men and obtained the best able-bodied
seamen the NMU had available; the first, second, and
third mates, the chief wireless operator, purser, and the
chief engineer, were black. For two and a half years Mulzac guided the *Booker T. Washington* through sub-infested
waters to deliver soldiers and war matériel to Europe.

Twelve other Liberty Ships were named after black
Americans and commanded by black captains. The S.S.
Douglass was torpedoed and sunk, but Captain Adrian
Richardson, originally of the Dutch West Indies (he also
received his Master's license in 1916 and was captain of
an Army transport in World War I), and his crew were
saved and all re-enlisted on another ship. They clearly
demonstrated that blacks could command large vessels
with mixed crews under difficult circumstances. Many
blacks have now graduated from the Merchant Marine
academies and several skipper freighters in the U.S. Merchant Marine.

Today blacks serve on every conceivable type of ship,
from supertankers to the lightships. When the lightship
Nantucket was run down, the five seamen who drowned
were Cape Verdean and the sixth was from Saint Helena.
In 1970 there were 8,918 Negroes employed in the offshore
maritime industry, approximately 7½ percent of the work
force. The largest number are employed in the Gulf re-
gion, where the black proportion of employees is 10.4 percent. They work on barges and lighters on the Mississippi
as well as on the new LASH and container ships.

VIII

Coastal Traders

Almost as soon as the colonists arrived in America they realized that transportation by sea was quicker than by land. Deep rivers and sheltered bays offered access to the hinterland as well as safe harbors. There was fine timber for boat-building almost everywhere, and pines provided pitch for waterproofing the seams of ships. Only cordage had to come from elsewhere. By 1640 Governor John Winthrop of Massachusetts had established trade with New York, Virginia, and the West Indies. His son owned land in Barbados, and in 1650 other slave-owning Barbados planters had purchased Shelter Island (then Farrell Island) off Long Island to provide food and barrel staves for their sugar plantations in the West Indies. By 1671 John Hull, goldsmith of Boston, had a fleet of ketches, small vessels forty to fify feet long, square-rigged on the mainmast with a lateen sail on the mizzenmast. Trade was with Jamaica, Virginia, and Campeche (now Yucatán and Belize). The crews were mixed black, white, and Indian, with English and Irish predominating.

For the next three hundred years the pattern of coastal trade was set. From the towns along the rivers of the northern states the ship would load dried and salted fish, lumber, and foodstuffs. From the southern states would come turpentine, cattle, and fuel, while the West Indies contributed salt, molasses, and tropical fruit to the trade.

The sailing conditions and the winds off the Atlantic coast of North America dictated the kind of ships needed. Most winds were from the west or southwest, with some northwest winds in the winter. In addition, the Gulf Stream flowed from southeast to northwest at three to five knots. Thus passage from the West Indies north was usually much faster than the return voyage. The advantage was so great that ships from Europe to New York sailed by way of the West Indies or Bermuda despite the longer distance. Going south meant either taking a chance on riding a northeastern storm wind, which might blow the ship far offshore, or hugging the coast in summer to take advantage of the warm land breezes by day and anchoring at night. Small ships with a fore-and-aft rig that could be pointed closer into an unfavorable wind would beat a square-rigger under these circumstances. Ships with shallow draft could also deliver their cargo direct to the docks of towns and plantations located on creeks and rivers without time-consuming transshipment. The number of towns along the eastern seaboard that classed themselves as seaports were legion.

Other considerations were the large, sheltered bodies of water on the coast—the Sounds of the Carolinas, the tremendous Chesapeake and Delaware bays, the Hudson River-Long Island Sound system, and the islands that shelter the New England coast. Only along Cape Hatteras, the Jersey shore, and at Cape Cod did ships have to sail on the open sea.

Deep-sea captains accused the coasters of navigating "by the bark of dogs," but sloops, schooners, and other small craft outnumbered the more spectacular square-riggers fifty to one. Coaster crews did not need well-trained sailors. Many a "master" was hazy on navigation by sextant. Even large rowboats, without navigators and manned by black plantation hands, were used as fast couriers between Carolina, Georgia, and New York. They traveled along the shore and did not depend on the wind.

Blacks had their share in the coastal trade, mostly as sailors but occasionally as captains and owners. The large number of small vessels and the almost perpetual shortage of crewmen made it easy for men from minority groups and social misfits to find a berth to "ship out" and escape from unpleasant conditions on shore. Very few coastal captains worried about the antecedents of their crewmen or the possession of proper papers. Ex-slaves, debtors, absconding husbands, and runaway boys could be found on the small vessels. Only in Maine did the poor economic conditions provide enough Yankees to man the coastal sailing ships, and even there death or desertion of the original crew members soon mixed the composition of the forecastle hands of the Maine ships.

Olaudah Equiano, or Gustavas Vargas as he was named by his master, left an interesting account of the early coasters. Originally he had been captured in Nigeria and had served as captain's servant and gunner in the British navy. In 1760 he was sold in Montserrat in the West Indies to a Mr. King, a Quaker who "loaded many vessels a year, especially to Philadelphia." Because of his sea experience, Equiano was placed in charge of a shallop or "morse boat" collecting sugar and molasses from plantations on Montserrat and other islands for transshipment on larger vessels. He then became a sailor, while still a slave, on a sixty-ton sloop trading between Montserrat, Saint Eustatius, and North American ports. Cargoes included molasses, "new" slaves, and fresh fruit. On one trip his captain made a 300 percent profit on a cargo of pork from Charleston to Philadelphia, and even more money on a cargo of cattle from Savannah, Georgia, to Montserrat. While the captain made money for himself and for Mr. King, Equiano started trading on his own. His first venture was a single three-pence glass tumbler carried from Saint Eustatius to Montserrat and sold for a 100 percent profit. Later he managed to carry small quantities of fresh fruit and once was given a tierce (forty-two gallons) of sugar to sell on his own account. Eventually Equiano earned enough money to buy his freedom from Mr. King. He later became a major figure in the anti-slavery movement in England and in the settlement of Sierra Leone by freed slaves.

Equiano also described a special hazard faced by black sailors. Planters in Charleston or Savannah, knowing that blacks had no standing in court, would haul a poor black sailor before a magistrate and swear that he was an escaped slave. The black was then condemned to be returned to his "owners" and quickly shipped off inland. He could not help himself since a black man's testimony was not listened to; nor would the sloop captain find out in time what happened to his crew member. Although Equiano escaped an attempt of this kind, one of his "free" shipmates lost his freedom in this manner. Equiano was unusual only in that he learned to read, write, and navigate, but black sailors, both free and slave, were common enough to cause no special mention in the chronicles of the time.

The small size of the ships in the coastal and West Indies trade is confirmed from customhouse records. A few examples will suffice:

"Brig *Peggy*, 50 tons and nine men, from Tortola to Annapolis, December 2, 1774, with 15 hogsheads of muscevado [refined sugar] and 12,800 lbs. brown sugar."

"Sloop *Betsy*, 35 tons and six men, from Hispaniola [Haiti] to Annapolis with 60 tierces sugar and 19 hogshead molasses."

Despite their small size, these ships were capable of very long voyages. The ninety-ton sloop *Lady Washington* helped open the Northwest fur trade on the Columbia River. The Hudson River sloop *Enterprise* was one of the first American ships in Canton, China. However, square-rigged ships did better than a fore-and-after on the long reaches before the trade winds, and the sloops and schooners were found primarily in the coastal trade.

During the Revolutionary War black sailors, even on merchant ships, faced special jeopardy. Any Negro on an American ship captured by the British was automatically assumed to be a slave and could be sold as "enemy property" along with the captured ship and cargo. If the black managed to produce papers proving he was not a slave, they were impounded as "court documents"; he was then left without papers and was subject to enslavement by anyone in Jamaica who cared to haul him in front of a magistrate. Negroes on British or Tory ships were handled the same way by French prize courts in Martinique and Haiti. Similar abuses occurred during the undeclared war with France and the War of 1812 as well as where blacks sailed under the flags of Haiti, Holland, or Denmark when those nations were classed as "enemy" during the Napoleonic wars.

Despite these risks the number of blacks in the coastal trade increased. Some rose to be mates, captains, and owners of small ships. By 1829 there was enough demand for blacks who could serve as officers that the African Free School in New York gave courses in navigation to twelve-year-old boys.

By 1830 severe social changes had taken place on land, but that did not disrupt the old trading circuit. In the northern United States slavery had become economically unprofitable and socially unacceptable. Legally, almost all blacks were free, although they were definitely not equal socially. This opened the way for those who wished to become sailors or who had acquired boats. Since the honorific "captain" and its implied social status was not given to any master of a small coaster, white society could accept the existence of black bosuns, mates, and pilots rather readily.

In the West Indies, too, slavery was gradually being abolished, although more of the social and economic restrictions were retained. Bermuda ended slavery in 1831 but retained the regulation that black-owned vessels were not permitted to be absent more than one day from shore when there was no white captain aboard. Black offshore fishermen became common, and the fishing boats served as training ground for crewmen for bigger sailing ships. The recognition of the free black nation of Haiti also implied the right to issue "captain's licenses," and many a West Indian acquired papers there even though he was born on a different island. At the same time the plantation-based sugar economy collapsed and new products replaced the loads of sugar. The demand for pineapples, citrus fruit, and other tropical products increased and gave free blacks a chance to prosper.

The southern United States provided the greatest change and the greatest tensions. Here the invention of the cotton gin had created a profitable industry, but one that required much hand labor. The planters felt this labor could only be supplied by black slaves. This in turn gave the South a stake in preserving and extending slavery and its corollary, the suppression of all free blacks, including sailors. The problem that the black seamen represented for the southern states can be judged from the restrictive regulations that were passed by the various state legislatures. In 1804 Virginia provided that no vessel could have more than one third of its crew black and allowed no black captains. Maryland stipulated that ships with an all-black crew must have a white pilot aboard since "so many slaves had escaped aboard vessels"; this covered fishermen as well as coastal traders. South Carolina law prohibited a free black from leaving his ship in any Carolina port under the threat of being immediately sold as an "absolute slave." In addition, federal officers such as customs inspectors became searchers for escaping slaves under the federal fugitive slave acts. These laws should have been sufficient to drive free blacks off the seas, but the fact that blacks needed jobs and the coastal trade could not find an alternative labor source meant that conditions continued much as before. Even in a southern port such as Petersburg, Virginia, the 1860 census showed that John Updike, a Negro, owned the sloops and schooners *Jolly Sailor, Two Brothers, Jannett,* and *William and Mary.* Another Negro boatman, Richard Parsons of Campbell County, owned several small boats. Of course, black owners were more common in New York and Pennsylvania than in the South, and blacks visiting southern ports had to be more circumspect than before passage of the restrictive laws.

The Civil War produced a great change in the composition of the U.S. Merchant Marine. Rebel raiders and U.S. blockading squadrons sank many larger ships. Other vessels were transferred to foreign registry, and still other sailing ships found that steamers had taken their market. However, despite an increase of inland population and railway building, the great industrial boom and the growth of the cities required carriers for more bulk cargo. Economics dictated that these coastal bulk carriers be powered by sail and wind rather than steam. Sixty-five percent of all U.S. coastal vessels were sailing ships as late as 1900.

On the high seas the famous clipper ships had been the last attempt to have sail compete with steam on the basis of speed and comfort, and sail had lost. Now sailing ships carried stone and lime for building as well as wood and coal for fueling the new industries and the new railroads. West Indian fruit and Bermuda onions were to be found on the tables of the newly rich, brought by sloop and schooner. Cheap rates was the watchword for the successful operation of coastal vessels. Pay was kept low and the work was hard. Expanding opportunities in fields easier than coastal shipping attracted labor, so there was an increasing shortage of sailors. Color prejudice was dispensed with; any male body, white or black, drunk or sober, skilled or unskilled, was taken aboard ship. "Bucko" mates and hard-fisted captains kept the motley crews in order and at work.

In the early days lumber had come from New England, but by the Civil War the northern forests were nearly exhausted. Southern pine replaced northern fir, both as building material and as firewood. Timber was loaded through special holes cut in the bow of the ship, and when the holds were full it was piled on deck so high that the helmsman sometimes could not see the bow of the boat. Timber prevented a ship from sinking, but the high deck load made handling sail dangerous. Turpentine and other explosive naval stores were often shipped on the same schooner as timber.

Blacks were very active in the South's lumber trade and often were hired to replace deserted seamen. In Gulfport, Mississippi, for instance, experienced white sailors were offered higher wages on Gulf fishing boats than on coasters, and often switched trades. They were then replaced by local blacks, many of whom were experienced either in the timber trade or as lightermen. These blacks might stay aboard the next trip or might just serve until they had earned enough money to buy their own schooners to enter the West Indian fruit trade. Both Biloxi and Gulfport had many black-owned ships around the turn of the century.

Logwood, a wood used for dying wool and silk black, was grown in Jamaica, Haiti, and Belize. It had been a

commercial cargo since the 1600's and remained a Caribbean export until World War II. Blocks of wood weighing
four hundred pounds were lightered out to the schooners
lying offshore and loaded by West Indian workers and the
North American blacks comprising the schooner crews.
Often Jamaicans and Haitians used this opportunity to obtain passage to the United States as crewmen or to become
full-time sailors.

Special mention should be made of the guano trade.
Guano is phosphate derived from bird droppings and is
found on islets. In 1856 the U.S. Congress passed a law
allowing anyone to mine guano from any uninhabited
islet or cay. Importation of guano was considered part of
the coastal trade for many years. Navassa Cay, a small
waterless islet between Cuba and Jamaica, became "almost
a suburb of Baltimore" and an anteroom of hell. It is said
that police magistrates offered minor offenders a choice
between working on Navassa or going to jail, with jail
being considered far preferable. Thus sailors who got into
fights, along with homeless men and other derelicts became
"voluntary" guano workers. Naturally these included a
fair number of blacks. On Navassa there was neither water
nor shade. Even the hard-shell officers did not go ashore,
conducting their business from the boats being loaded in
the surf. The trade only ended when the accumulated de-
posit was worked out.

In 1881 the Chesapeake and Ohio Railroad laid tracks
to the pierside at Newport News, Virginia. From that time
on, Newport News was the loading port for coal. Schooners
were loaded with coal from chutes, with hull "trimmers,"
usually blacks, bent double under the deck beams to shovel

the cargo into all corners of the hold. Pay was small: eight cents an hour plus beer money to wash the dust out of one's throat. When the coal was sent to the West Indies, it was unloaded by black women who carried it in baskets on their heads. This coal was not used for domestic purposes on the islands but was held to sell to visiting steamships and for factories.

Cotton was another favorite bulk cargo, although inland steamers offered stiff competition on shipping rates. Loading cotton brought better pay than serving as sailors and offered whites an inducement to "jump ship." Replacements in southern ports were usually blacks.

In November 1936 the *Doris Hamlin* sailed from Baltimore with a crew of eight: captain, engineer, bosun, cook, and four seamen. The cook and the seamen were blacks, the captain and engineer were white regulars, and Robert Burgess, photographer and author, served as bosun and left us a record of this trip. From Baltimore the *Hamlin* sailed down to Newport News to load coal, then waited for two days for a favorable wind to Bermuda. After unloading at Bermuda they ran empty to Haiti, where they loaded logwood. It took several days to load both chunks and the four-hundred-pound logs, and the pictures show black Americans and black Haitians working together. Then the *Hamlin* sailed back to Baltimore. About the same time the *Parnell T. White* with a black crew came into Baltimore carrying salt from Turks Island, loaded coal for the West Indies, and returned with a cargo of mahogany wood from Georgetown, Guyana, to New York. The *G. A. Kohler*, another schooner built during World War I, sailed at this time with a load of bricks to Tampa, Florida, and returned with phosphates As long as the schooners and sloops found cargo, they tramped between the ports of the eastern seaboard and the Caribbean.

Around 1850 some of the schooners began to be built much larger than before. To facilitate handling the increased sail areas, schooners were designed with three and more masts, finally ending with a seven-masted absurdity. Crews, however, remained small. A nine-hundred-ton schooner carried a crew of eight, about the same as an eighty-ton brig of a century earlier. "A man, a boy, and an idiot" were considered adequate to handle the ninety-ton *Pioneer*. Long hours were the rule, not only at sea but also loading and unloading in port. When one of the crewmen of a schooner unloading bricks complained that the sun had long set, the captain sang out, "Keep going, there will be another one up soon." Maintenance was skimpy; report after report talked about rotten canvas and frayed rigging. On some large schooners "donkey" steam engines were installed to load and unload and to hoist the large sails, but that meant money for coal and wages for an engineer. Most ships dispensed with such "luxuries," simply driving their crews harder. Photographs of the time show how many of those hard-driven crews were black.

As early as 1840 almost all of the coastal and river passenger traffic was handled by paddle-wheel steamer. Paddle wheels were clumsy in a heavy sea and the engine consumed tons of expensive coal, but they were ideal for fast, comfortable, reliable service in sheltered water. Luxurious day or night boats carried passengers from Baltimore to Norfolk, from Albany to New York City, from New York City up the Long Island Sound to Boston. Paddle steamers equipped with stern paddles also operated on inland rivers and lakes. In each case they replaced passenger-carrying sloops and schooners, since passenger fares paid for the high cost of fuel. The high demands of these well-paying passengers also created employment opportunities for many blacks. The competing shipping lines offered fine food and excellent service. Blacks who were trained as waiters, cooks, and servants on the plantations of the South were the first to sense this opening; in turn, they trained others until practically the whole service department of the coastal passenger ships was manned by blacks. Other blacks were hired as stokers and coal heavers in the hot engine rooms, since the belief existed at the time that blacks could stand more heat than whites. From stoker to engineer was only a short step. Still other blacks used the knowledge they had gained as fishermen and schoonermen to become pilots, guiding the ships around obstructions and shifting sand banks. The "officers," dressed in plenty of gold braid, were always white, but much of the working of the ship from bridge to keel was entrusted to blacks.

In the West Indies, sloops and schooners are still seen working at their old trades. Groups of them carry fruit and lumber from Venezuela to the Netherlands Antilles. Others handle general cargo in the Grenadines or sail between Tobago and the Virgin Islands. Some of these are converted Gloucester and Lunenburg fishing schooners; others were built in the West Indies and are manned by local sailors, blacks whose families have been sailors for generations.

The last U.S. sailing ships were laid up during World War II, when seamen were desperately needed to man the

newly built Liberty and Victory ships. After the war, however, some of the sailing vessels were refurbished or newly
built to satisfy a sense of history. Some of them are sailing
as "dude" cruisers, carrying vacationers who hanker after
a bygone era without wishing to know about the hard work
or danger. Other schooners are tied up as displays at marine
museums or serve as training vessels. On many of these
the role that blacks played in our maritime history is beginning to be rediscovered.

~~~~~~

IX

Whalers

"B-l-o-w-s, b-l-o-w-s." The cry of the lookout on a whaling ship meant a rush of the crew from the forecastle to the boats. The men who made up these crews probably had the most diverse backgrounds of those in any trade. Blacks from New England and West Africa and the West Indies, Yankees and Gay Head Indians, Irish and Polynesians—all were to be found on the ships that made their livelihood from hunting the large mammals. When a whaling ship got to within about two miles of a whale, the boats were lowered and manned. Moving silently by sail and paddles, they approached the unsuspecting prey until the harpooner was close enough to hurl his weapon into the whale's body, making the boat fast to the quarry. The harpooner then changed places with the officer in the boat, who handled the eighteen-foot killing lance and the bomb gun. Sometimes the whale died quietly but often he "sounded," diving to get away from his tormentors. A sperm whale could stay submerged about an hour, then had to surface to breathe, the blast of moist air forming the "spout." Again the whaleboat rowed in close to have the officer plunge the lance once more into the blubber-coated body. Then it was "stern all, for your lives" as the boat backed off to avoid being smashed by the giant flukes of a whale in its death flurry. Sometimes the harpoon or lance changed the whale into the nightmare of all whalers—a fighting whale. With tail, flukes, and teeth the enraged animal attacked his deadly enemy, the whaleboat. The boat could be smashed into its component planks in a second, killing crew members almost incidentally. Or crew members could be left floundering in the water to be rescued by other boats, or drowned, or attacked by sharks as their luck would have it. The sharp blades and the running rope might also kill a whaleman, and there was hardly a log of a whaling voyage that did not record one or more deaths from these causes. This was not a sport but the occupation of many blacks.

After the danger of the hunt itself came the drudgery. When the whale was finally dead, "fin out" as the whalers called it, the body had to be towed back to the ship. "Of all the ungainly things to tow," said an old whaleman, "a dead sperm whale is the worst. You could stick your oar two, three times into the same hole in the ocean before making any progress." When the dead whale was next to the ship, heavy chains were hooked to the body and the work of "trying out" began. This was a job where the officers worked almost harder than the men, for the mates were standing on a narrow plank "stage" swung out from the bulwarks. With sharp "spades" they separated the giant head from the body and stripped off the heavy blubber. A couple of barrels of fine spermaceti oil could be dipped out of the head, but the blubber had to be boiled to extract

the oil. The fires under the "trying out" kettles were fueled
by scraps of blubber from the whale. For a day or more
after catching the whale the crew would toil, covered with
oil and choked with smoke. Then they were ready to lower
the boats once more.

There were, of course, weeks and even months when no
whales were sighted. Then the monotony, poor food, and
lack of privacy brought differences to the fighting point.
Yet despite the danger and the boredom, there were no
records of fights conducted on racial lines. There might
be name calling, there was often the feeling that the captain preferred one racial or national group over another,
but whaling was a truly integrated trade.

Hard work, poor pay, and voyages that lasted up to three
years made whalers unpopular with professional sailors, so
crews were comprised of men who could not get other
berths, men planning to become officers, green hands, men
"shanghaied" with drink or blackjack, and crews recruited
from islands in every ocean of the world.

Whaling in America was multiracial from its very beginning. Rowing boats and small sloops operating inshore
in the 1600's were manned by a high percentage of Indians
from Long Island and Nantucket with an increasing number of blacks joining in. In 1715 the first ship to mount
"try-works" on board instead of on shore made the ships
independent of land. Soon whalemen followed the whales
wherever they could be found. By 1765 American ships
were whaling off the Cape Verde Islands and the west coast
of Africa; by 1788 they were in the Pacific, and by 1823
they were ranging from Antarctica to Greenland.

By 1807 one third of the crews of whalers sailing out of

Nantucket were blacks, living in a section called "Guinea-Town" or "New Guinea." The following is a specimen of a crew list and the "lays" they were paid in that year: "Captain $\frac{1}{8}$ share, first mate $\frac{1}{20}$th, second mate $\frac{1}{37}$th, two boat steerers [harpooners] $\frac{1}{48}$th each, cooper $\frac{1}{60}$th, five men $\frac{1}{75}$th each, boy $\frac{1}{120}$, five black men $\frac{1}{80}$th each, one black man $\frac{1}{80}$th on 400 barrels, one black man $\frac{1}{90}$th, one black man $\frac{1}{85}$th."

A $\frac{1}{80}$th share would have come to about $400 gross, but there would have been deductions for clothes and tobacco drawn from the "slop chest," for hiring expenses, and for other items. The black sailor probably got only $100 for his work during the entire voyage. Even this pay was considered to be overly generous in the later days of the whaling industry when "lays" dropped to $\frac{1}{200}$th for a green hand and deductions included anything and everything the captain or the owners could think of. Returning whalermen were lucky to get money for one good spree ashore.

As the nineteenth century went on there was an increasing demand for whale oil. More and more whalers were fitted out. Twenty thousand men formed the crews of some seven hundred ships in the 1850's. The Civil War period put an end to the whale oil boom. In 1859 the first oil well was drilled in Pennsylvania, and kerosene or "coal oil" started to replace oil from whales. During the war itself the Confederate raiders *Shenandoah* and *Alabama* together sank some fifty whalers. Another forty aging whalers were bought by the U.S. Government to sink in the exits of Confederate harbors as part of the "stone fleet." This was followed by a disaster in the Arctic where thirty-three whalers were caught in the ice and crushed in 1871. Although the crews escaped the ice, the ships were lost and not replaced.

The whaling industry entered a period of ruthless cost cutting. "Lays" dropped, prices from the slop chest were set at unreasonably high levels, and food quality went from bad to nearly inedible. Desertion by crew members became common, and sometimes captains abandoned crewmen on the way home or hazed them into desertion in order to pocket their wages. At other times supplies were bought but paid for "with a loose topsail"—the ship sailed away without paying for the goods.

Because of this cost cutting, whaling ships only touched land on small islands where desertion was difficult. These places allowed the ship to pick up fresh water and vegetables and gave their crews a chance to have a spell ashore, perhaps to convince some islanders to join the crew temporarily or for the entire voyage. The Cape Verde Islands were favorite stops for rest and recruiting, as were Annobón Island (now part of Equatorial Guinea), Dominica, and Barbados. Other stops included Saint Helena, Mauritius, various Polynesian islands, New Zealand, and the Seychelles. In some of these places, as well as in Honolulu, Hawaii, whalers off-loaded oil into freighters and tenders, allowing the whalers to stay out for four years without "paying off."

Under those circumstances less than one third of the crews that started a voyage ever completed it. Some died, some deserted, some were left ashore deliberately. Anyone who gave the promise of becoming a good whaleman had no difficulty in shipping as a harpooner on his second voyage. Harpooners ranked as officers, and it was easy to advance from there to mate even without formal schooling. Reports again and again mention mates who could not write up a log or navigate with a sextant but were given the rating and respect of an officer nonetheless. Cape Verdeans, Azoreans, and blacks from the United States made up a larger and larger proportion of the crew. First they were only crewmen, then officers, and finally captains and owners.

Whalers were familiar with much of the world. Pyrrhus Cance, an ex-slave from Southampton, Long Island, was a harpooner on the whaler *Manhattan,* which visited Yedo Harbor (now Tokyo) eight years before Commodore Perry opened Japan to the world in 1853. Although none of the Americans was permitted to land, the visiting Japanese aboard the *Manhattan* were amazed at the black skin of Cance and gave him many gifts. A North American black became chief of the Polynesian island of Fanuva. When another chief made war on him, Sam (no other name is recorded) shipped on a whaler to get the guns to put down his rival. Whalers traded with West African villagers and with Eskimos, Seychelles islanders, and people from Madagascar. In 1901, for example, the whaler *Mermaid* dropped anchor off the African village of Baraco (Ghana). "Each man ransacked his chest or sea bag and unearthed trinkets of various kinds. There were needles and thread, hooks and lines, dominoes and rings made from whale teeth. . . . Sea shells, grass mats, fruits, goats, pigs and chickens proved to be all the villagers had in the way of barter." The list of equipment for a first-class whale ship for a voyage around Cape Horn published in 1874 includes goods for "recruits or trade": "19 bales cotton cloths, 36 dz. pairs of shoes of various kinds, 50 boxes of soap and 1000 pounds of tobacco."

The story of William T. Shorey, a Barbadian-born black, illustrates the career of many another black whaleman. In 1876 he shipped as a green hand out of Provincetown, Cape Cod, Massachusetts, on a whaler and returned from that trip with the rank of harpooner. On his next cruise he signed on as third mate on the *Emma F. Herriman,* returning with her to San Francisco in 1880 as first mate. Six years later he was her captain, the only black captain on the Pacific coast. In 1889 Shorey became captain of the whaler *Alexander* but lost her three years later in the Pribilof Islands of the Arctic. He received command of another whaler, the *Andrew Hicks.* This was no sinecure, for her old captain had quit after writing: "The old *'Hicks'* is getting mighty shaky . . . her rigging is in terrible shape and I expect her mainmast to go overboard any day. She has the same old leaks. . . ." Storey managed to get eight more successful voyages out of the old boat before he retired.

Not all whaling stories ended so happily. In 1819 the whaling ship *Essex* left Nantucket for a voyage in the South Pacific. After various vicissitudes she was attacked by a sperm whale and sunk. The story of that sinking was published in Boston in 1821 and formed the base for Herman Melville's epic *Moby Dick.* What was not used by Melville is the second part of the story of the crew of the *Essex.* After the whale sank the ship there were twenty survivors aboard three boats, six of them blacks. The boats drifted around the South Atlantic for months, touching at an uninhabited island where three crew members stayed rather than chance more voyaging. The three boats went on with two blacks in each boat. As food ran out two whites and four blacks died, one after the other. Only one man was buried in the sea. The others were eaten by the starving survivors. The second mate's boat with the two other blacks and some whites disappeared without trace, but the other two boats with six survivors were picked up. The three castaways were also rescued.

On the east coast of America more and more whaling ships drifted into the hands of Cape Verdeans, both as captains and owners. These, in turn, recruited relatives and townsmen from the islands to join them. Wages on a whaler might be poor by American standards, but they were riches indeed compared to those available in the Cape Verde Islands. Another inducement to signing up on a whaler was that the ship "paid off" in New Bedford, Massachusetts. Immigration authorities did not check incoming sailors, and many of the Portuguese-speaking residents of New Bedford and Fall River originally settled in America after a whaling voyage. Some whaling ships ended their career as Cape Verde "packets" whose prime purpose was to bring in immigrants.

The last sail whaling ships went out of business in the 1920's. The *Charles W. Morgan* was laid up in 1921, the *Viola* sank in 1919, and the era ended when the old *Wanderer* went aground off Nantucket in 1923

While the bluff-bowed whaling ships sought their prey in the distant seas, any whale nearing the coast was fair game for shore-based boats. In some cases, such as on the coasts of Japan, Chile, and Alaska, fast "killer" steamers were used. Off Long Island, New York, off Beaufort, South

Carolina, off Cape Cod, Massachusetts, and off the West
Indies, shore whaling represented an additional source of
income rather than a full-time business. Migrating schools
of blackfish, each good for a barrel of oil, were systemati-
cally herded into the shallows to die and were then boiled
down. Stranded whales were also stripped of their blubber
and baleen. Blacks and whites participated in exploiting
these occasional bonanzas.

In the West Indies, shore whaling was closer to the
methods used on the American mainland in Colonial days.
When a spout was sighted from land, two or more whaleboats were launched. These craft might have been acquired
from homebound whaling ships or have been built locally.
Black whalers had shown their fellow islanders all the necessary skills. The islanders used hand harpoons and lances
instead of the more expensive harpoon bombs. In the case
of a successful kill, one of the black whalemen swam over
despite the presence of sharks and attached a line through
the tail of the whale, which was then towed home in tri-
umph. Blubber and whalebone belonged to the crew of the
whaleboats and was sold, but the meat was often distrib-
uted free to anyone who wanted it. Whaling was carried
on in this manner in Bermuda, Trinidad, and Bequia (now
part of Saint Vincent). The blacks of Bequia were the last
West Indian whalers, bringing in two right whales as late
as 1974.

X

The Cape Verdean Packet Trade

On January 10, 1970, a three-masted schooner left New Bedford, Massachusetts, for Africa under sail, continuing a tradition of daring and courage that had linked the peoples of New England and the Cape Verde Islands for over one hundred years. Like many of her predecessors, the leaky *Tina Maria* sank in rough seas, having relied upon Cape Verdean seamanship and favorable weather to bring goods and a seventy-eight-year-old passenger to the homeland of three hundred thousand New Englanders off the coast of West Africa. Cape Verdeans are a mulatto people mixed by centuries of sea contact.

Since the end of the eighteenth century, New England whalers had stopped in the Cape Verde archipelago to pick up the renowned seamen of the islands. Merchant ships in the nineteenth century brought back salt, hides, and the major export of the island—its hard-working people, to work in the cranberry bogs and factories of New England. Cape Verdean seamen later bought their own vessels to take goods and people between the United States and Cape

Verde. Often they would be advanced the necessary money to purchase an old vessel by the owners of the textile mills and cranberry fields if they would bring back a certain number of workers.

Antonio Coelho was the first Cape Verdean-American to purchase a vessel to enable his people to travel and send goods back to the islands, and to pick up new immigrants. He bought the *Nellie May,* a sixty-four-ton fishing schooner, hired an old whaleman as captain, and sailed in 1892 from Providence for Brava. Fifty people paid fifteen dollars each for the passage. Only a few days out, the captain died of a heart seizure. The mate did not know anything about navigation but tried to steer a course in the general direction of Cape Verde. After a month at sea they encountered a steamer and were told they had passed the islands and were five hundred miles south of the archipelago. Forty-five days after leaving Providence they reached the harbor of Furna on Brava Island. Coelho hired a new captain and sailed back with the *Nellie May* to Providence in the spring of the next year. There were 117 passengers and crew aboard, and the schooner arrived in twenty-eight days.

The *Nellie May* made another round-trip with Captain José Godinho in command. The passage to the Cape Verde Islands took ninety days—one of the most terrible on record for its length and the suffering endured. Food and water ran out; two of the crew went mad and jumped overboard. The captain felt he had not been properly compensated for his troubles, and it is said he deliberately beached the ship so he could buy the *Nellie May* at auction as a derelict.

One of the famous captains of the Cape Verde packet trade was John Sousa of Brava. At age six he lost his father. His mother was too poor to care for him, so he went to live with his uncle, Captain John Zurich of São Nicolau. Zurich taught him sailing and navigation, and at age twelve Sousa was running a small boat between the islands with his cousins. At eighteen he was made captain of one of Zurich's ships that traveled to America. For most of the next forty years he made annual trips to New England and carried salt to Gambia, wood and rice from Bissau, and passengers to Dakar.

In 1924 he took his family to America on the *William Grabner* and lived there for fourteen months before he was denounced by fellow Cape Verdeans for bringing in immigrants illegally. He had to leave quickly on the first ship available.

The family was finally reunited in São Vicente, but Captain John often gave his family cause to worry. Once he was considered lost after three months at sea between America and São Nicolau. Another time while sailing the *Atlanta* to the United States he lost two masts and the rudder in a storm, jury-rigged a sail and steering device, and made his way back to Cape Verde. At yet another time, between Cape Verde and Bermuda, a cyclone hit his ship and he had to abandon it, but was rescued by a passing boat. He lost still another ship on her maiden voyage between São Vicente and São Nicolau.

He was described by people who knew him as very courageous and calm in adversity. At the age of fifty-six he retired from the sea and established a small farm on the island of Fogo, but kept up his shipping business. On his death bed at age seventy-five in 1958, he was still "fighting the wind and the sea" and calling his cousin to "pull in the sheets because the wind was picking up."

One of Captain John's good friends was Henry Rose.

Captain Rose made his first trip from Brava to America in 1911 at age thirteen as a messboy. Eleven years later he was made master of the schooner *Volante*. In the middle of the Atlantic, while a greenhorn was at the wheel, the boat jibed and the swinging boom knocked Rose overboard. None of the crew knew what to do, and for twenty minutes Rose hung on to the logline and shouted instructions. Finally, after spending two hours swimming in the cold Atlantic, Rose was rescued after the crew managed to turn the schooner. Nonetheless, the *Volante* reached Saint Vincente in nineteen days—record time.

Henry Rose had his best days aboard the old schooner *Valkyria*, a two-masted former whaler he commanded from 1923 to 1926. He made fourteen crossings in her, and claims he made one voyage in twelve days. She was solidly built, as she proved in the 1923 crossing when for ten days she battled a hurricane. Rose jettisoned fifty tons of cargo, but arrived safely in Brava with his thirty-two passengers— forty-five days at sea. On April 8, 1924, the *Valkyria* and her rival, the *Yukon,* sailed from Brava together and arrived the same day, May 13, in Providence. Captain Benjamin Costa, former master of the *Valkyria,* was captain of the *Yukon.* For the return voyage, a wager of $1,500 was arranged for the fastest vessel. The two craft and the *William A. Graber* under Captain John Sousa, left Providence on October 19, 1924. The *Valkyria* carried seven passengers and seventeen seamen, while the *Yukon* had fifteen passengers and twenty-six crew members. The *Valkyria* won, arriving on November 13, and remained the indisputed "Queen of the Cape Verde Packets" until 1926 when she dismasted.

During the night of November 5, 1926, the *Valkyria* struck a derelict. The collison brought down the foremast and eventually the mainmast, and opened the stem. Captain Rose tried to hack away the rigging and masts, which were pounding against the sides of the ship. Two seamen were swept overboard during this operation. For two days the ship drifted, a helpless wreck; finally her crew of fifteen and two young girls were rescued by a passing British tanker.

Captain Rose then took over the *Manta*, the last of the New Bedford whaling ships. He made five trips with her. The worst trip was in January 1928, when she ran into such bad calms that it took fifty-three days from Providence to the islands.

In 1929, seventeen-year-old John J. Barros sailed the *Manta* back but ran her aground off Nantucket. Two trawlers pulled the *Manta* off the Nantucket Shoals and towed her to Vineyard Haven. The Coast Guard, suspecting illegal immigrants, sent agents aboard and discovered eleven unfortunate aliens hiding below decks in the bilges. The *Manta* was fined and auctioned off. Captain Albertino J. Senna bought her, and she continued in the island packet trade for several years. In 1934, Captain Senna brought the *Manta* to Providence. After a summer spent refitting and rerigging the old ship, she sailed from Providence for Brava on November 8, 1934, with a crew of nineteen and a passenger list of thirteen, including three women and six children, plus one guernsey heifer. A week before Christmas, the newspapers noted that the *Manta* was thirty-nine days out of Providence and unreported "but supposedly winging her way to Brava." By mid-January the relatives and friends began to worry, for no word had been received from Cape Verde that she had arrived. Two packets, the *Winnepesauke* and the *Trenton,* had also sailed from New Bedford and had failed to reach Brava. The *Trenton,* an old New York pilot schooner, eventually made port, but the *Winnepesauke* was lost with all hands. The last hope for the *Manta* and her passengers was abandoned on February 24, 1935, when the vessel had been missing 107 days.

Another great tragedy was the loss of the *Mathilde.* In 1943 a group of young men in Cape Verde bought the fifty-five-foot sloop in order to sail to New England and there volunteer to fight for the United States during World War II. After only minimal repairs were made to the one-masted craft, they set sail from Brava on August 21, 1943. Humberto Balla, then age twelve, intended to accompany his older brother on the overloaded vessel, but when he saw the boat was already leaking, he jumped off before it had gotten far out of the harbor. It took him thirty minutes to swim ashore. He looked back and saw the sloop disappearing over the horizon. He wept, for he knew his compatriots were exposing themselves to certain death. September is the hurricane season and it is believed that the ship with her twenty brave volunteers went down in rough weather near Bermuda.

Cape Verdean skippers continued to make the hazardous crossing. One of those who persevered was John B. Costa, who had been aboard the *Manta* on an earlier voyage. One day while casting off, the shore line snapped and cut off Costa's right hand. It was twenty-nine hours before the *Manta* returned to port. By that time his mangled arm had become infected and had to be amputated. But this did not prevent him from going to sea again; in fact, he rose to become captain of several vessels, including the *Corona,* a handsome Herreshoff-designed steel sloop, and the *Capitana,* which had retraced Columbus's route to America for Harvard University before entering the Cape Verde packet trade. In 1945 John Costa bought the *Lucy Evelyn,* the last commercially operated three-masted schooner in New England, for $12,000. He had her refitted with a new deckhouse for more passenger accommodations, and announced he would take general cargo and passengers for $150 to Cape Verde. At first there was trouble obtaining sufficient cargo to make the trip profitable, but slowly it came: thirteen thousand feet of pine lumber and twenty tons of cement for a new church in Praia, a piano, household goods for the pastor (a South Dakotan who declined the sea voyage), two hundred drums of kerosene, three automobiles, canned food, and bundles of clothing for relatives in Cape Verde. Two paying passengers signed on, including Mrs. Teresa Neves, age sixty, whose sister had gone down with the *Mauta.* None of the crew of twelve had ever served on a sailing vessel.

As no one would go aloft and the captain had only one arm, the topsails could not be set. On May 9, 1946, the *Evelyn* was towed out of New Bedford Harbor. She arrived safely in Cape Verde thirty-four days later.

The return to the United States was a real test of Costa's ability and endurance. He left from Dakar on September 20 with ten women and five children among the passengers, a "crew" of twenty-eight, and 250 tons of salt. When she was in the middle of the Atlantic a heavy gale smashed the rudder and brought down the mizzenboom. Costa worked feverishly to improvise an apparatus of wires to work the crippled rudder. The *Evelyn* was only 280 miles from Block Island, Rhode Island, when a second storm struck on November 5, driving her back to a point 250 miles east of Currituck, North Carolina. Unable to hold course, the *Evelyn* was finally picked up by the Coast Guard and towed into Norfolk, Virginia, on November 22, after sixty-three days at sea.

The *Evelyn* was repaired and on February 15, 1947, set out for New Bedford. On February 21 she was in sight of the Vineyard Sound Lightship. Captain Costa, who had been on deck much of the time, turned in for a nap. Suddenly a blinding blizzard hit. Visibility dropped to zero in minutes. The howling northeast wind shredded the mainsail and the jib in rapid succession. Captain Costa ran for deep water under the foresail alone, and before the winter gale was over the *Evelyn* found herself off the Georges Banks. On February 27 the Coast Guard cutter *Legare* picked her up and started towing her back. Rough seas caused the towline to part several times. On March 2 the *Legare* was relieved by the larger cutter *Algonquin,* but as they approached Gay Head, another winter gale struck. In the early morning hours of March 3, four miles west of Cuttyhunk, the towline broke again and the *Algonquin* lost the *Evelyn* in the blizzard. On her own in raging seas before sixty-mile-an-hour winds, the *Evelyn* was drifting into shoal waters. Captain Costa ordered the anchor dropped, but the chain broke immediately. A second anchor held half a mile from the beach off Mattapoisett. The next morning, after the storm had finally ended, a tug towed her to New Bedford City Pier, arriving six months after she had set out from Cape Verde.

In late June the *Evelyn* set out for Cape Verde with ten passengers and a general cargo. The elements were kind to Captain Costa on that voyage, but the trip to the United States the next year was similar to the earlier ones. In March 1948 he left Praia for New Bedford via Dakar with seven paying passengers and twenty inexperienced crew members. The stop was planned at Dakar to drop the passengers off, but the winds prevented her eastward journey. Captain Costa discharged the passengers at Fogo and headed for America directly. Soon after leaving, a storm opened up a seam in her bow; there was no gas for the pump and the crew had to pump by hand the entire way across the Atlantic. A month out of Cape Verde the flour ran out, and by the time she reached New Bedford on April 12, 1948, most of the other food was also gone. Upon arrival the crew sued for wages. Costa had had only misfortunes with the *Evelyn* and sold the schooner for $1,550.

John B. Pontes, a Cape Verdean-American businessman, decided carrying cargo to Cape Verde could still be profitable, despite knowing of Costa's problems. In November 1946 he bought the steel luxury yacht *Illyria,* which had been pressed into Coast Guard service during World War II and was now considered surplus. She was a fine Italian-built vessel designed in 1928 for Cornelius Crane. Pontes renamed her *Madalan,* had her rerigged and the partitions ripped out below decks for cargo space, and hired Captain Oliveira Crus, a Cape Verde native who had handled a six-masted schooner.

The *Madalan* left Providence on June 8, 1947, with

twenty passengers plus live geese and pigs. It was a calm crossing that took seventy-four days before arrival in Cape Verde. She had a new engine, but Pontes would not allow it to be used because it was too expensive to operate!

The return voyage to Providence was a good deal faster, taking only thirty-nine days from Dakar to Providence, with twenty passengers and five barrels of rope tobacco, her only cargo. After staying in New England for Christmas and New Year, she attempted a winter crossing in January 1948. Five days out of port the *Madalan* ran into a week of gales that drove her 130 miles a day with no sails. Apart from three kerosene drums and a barrel of beef which were washed overboard, the brigantine came through without damage.

The *Madalan* was back in Providence on July 27, 1948, with forty-two passengers after making a forty-eight-day crossing from Dakar despite seventeen days of calm. In order to have fresh meat during the voyage, a stock pen had been built under the forecastle for four hogs, four cows, and thirty-seven sheep. Every year thereafter the *Madalan* returned in July and left in autumn after the cranberry harvest, when many Cape Verdean cranberry pickers would book passage home to visit family and friends. The comfortable conditions aboard the *Madalan* had made her a popular ship. In 1951 the *Madalan* carried forty-eight passengers and was crammed with baggage and cargo. Second Mate John Baptiste, Jr., boasted, "She's the finest ship ever to sail in the trade."

During her twenty-one-day run to Providence in 1953, two men, a passenger and a supercargo, died on board, and were buried at sea. On the trip back to Cape Verde in

January 1954, the mate John Brites was washed overboard by a wave; the next wave washed him back aboard, unhurt! Good fortune indeed smiled on the *Madalan* until she was sold in 1955.

The rival of the *Madalan* was the *Ernestina,* a two-masted schooner owned and operated by Henrique Mendes, who had been involved in the Cape Verde trade longer than anyone else. At age eighteen he ran away from his home in Fogo and sailed for New Bedford on the schooner *Serpa Pinto,* arriving May 2, 1898. In Providence he shoveled coal at twenty-six cents an hour for several months, then decided to ship out on a whaler. Thirteen dollars for six months labor proved too little money for Mendes. He left whaling and alternately worked as a deckhand aboard coastal schooners, took odd jobs ashore, kept a store in Wareham, or picked cranberries. People thought "he lived to save his money." After five years in the United States he made an agreement with a cranberry bog owner to bring forty contract workers form Cape Verde and was advanced the rest of the money needed to purchase his first vessel. Mendes would go on to own thirty different vessels in succession, all old and dilapidated. Several were lost in the Atlantic—the *William A. Grosier* 1914, *Ernest T. Lee* 1919, *Charles L. Jeffrey* 1927, and *Frank Brainerd* 1935. Each time a vessel sank, Mendes and his crew and passengers were rescued by passing steamers. Mendes would then go back to work ashore to save money for another vessel. He once bought the old barkentine *Savoya* for $8,000 in Baltimore and sold her a few years later for $15,000. While he had her, "She carry plenty passengers, make plenty money."

World War II halted the Cape Verde packet trade. As soon as the war was over, Henrique Mendes bought the famous Arctic exploration ship *Effie Morrissey,* which had sunk in Flushing, New York. The old schooner was raised and sold to Henrique's daughter-in-law, Louisa Mendes, for $7,000. Henrique repaired her in New Bedford and rechristened her *Ernestina.* For the next twenty years she sailed regularly between Providence and Cape Verde. The seasonal arrival of the *Madalan* and the *Ernestina* timed to coincide with the harvest of the cranberries was a joyous occasion for the Cape Verdeans of New England. Hundreds would come to the dock to greet the vessels, hear the news about friends living in the islands, and celebrate aboardship drinking sugarcane "grog" and dancing to the "mornas" played by the crew. The *Ernestina* would receive goods all summer for shipment to relatives in the islands. In autumn the community would come to the docks to bid a tearful farewell to these two brave ships which for so long served as the living link between their homeland and their newly adopted country.

Henrique Mendes was almost killed by a falling spar on one voyage; another time the *Ernestina* ran into two hurricanes; once she limped into Providence with a broken engine and almost no remaining fresh water or supplies. However, Mendes kept coming every year. Each year beginning in 1955 he said he would retire. He had made fifty-three Atlantic crossings and returned two more times in 1956 and 1957. He finally retired to his farm in Fogo at age eighty.

In 1959 Cecilio Andrade decided to take his schooner, the *Maria Sony,* to the United States. She was the former *Dorothy Snow,* which had won the Canadian fishing schooner races in 1912 and 1914. Still a fast ship, she reached Bermuda in twelve days. A hurricane then struck and she had to ride out the storm under bare poles. She finally reached Newport on July 25 and was towed to Providence by a tug. Ninety minutes after debarking, one of the passengers had a baby, which was named after the vessel.

After an overhaul and installation of a new engine in New Bedford, the *Maria Sony* sailed on November 7, 1959, for Cape Verde. Within a week the engine broke down; on November 20 rough seas broke the steering gear and the *Maria Sony* drifted helpless in a gale. On November 24 a giant wave crashed over the deck and broke nine beams. The crew now feared for the structural integrity of the vessel and used only a small triangular sail, threw over barrels of fuel and other cargo to lighten the ship, and prayed. For fifteen days she was buffeted about by waves, her mechanical pump broken, slowly sinking. Finally, on December 11, a freighter spotted her and started towing the old schooner to Bermuda. She was finally taken by the U.S. Coast Guard to St. George's Island. There Cecilio Andrade's troubles only began. Penniless, with a derelict schooner and a crew who refused to continue, Andrade stayed for ten months living from the generosity of local charity. Money was collected from Cape Verdian groups in the United States, and through the donated services and material in Bermuda, Andrade was able to put his boat back together and sail for Cape Verde. On November 10, 1960, the *Maria Sony* arrived in Cape Verde one year after her departure from New Bedford. Andrade never attempted another voyage to the United States.

In 1964 the *Ernestina* reappeared in Narragansett Bay.

Hundreds of sightseers and Cape Verdean families rushed to the Municipal Wharf in Providence to welcome the last survivor of the Cape Verde packet trade. She returned once more in 1965 to New Bedford. For the next ten years she was used in interisland trade in Africa. In 1976 she attempted the transatlantic crossing to join the Bicentennial Parade of Ships in New York Harbor as the only African participant. She dismasted in a storm shortly after leaving Cape Verde, but fortunately none of her all-Cape Verdean crew was injured. Efforts are now underway to preserve the historic schooner as a sail training vessel for young Cape Verdean-Americans and as a reminder of the Cape Verdean maritime heritage of courage and seamaneship.

XI

Menhaden Men

In the gray dawn the menhaden ship *Tideland* was ghosting along at three knots. Two miles off the starboard bow was the Delaware shore, just beginning to show in the morning light. Below deck the fishermen, all blacks from around Reedsville, Virginia, were having breakfast—ham, grits, scrambled eggs, juice, and coffee. Suddenly the klaxon horn cut through the conversation signaling the sighting of fish, a school of menhaden swimming near the surface. Within three minutes both seine boats were manned and in the water. Reeling out the seine net behind them, the boats separated to surround the dark patch of water that marked the presence of the school of fish. When the circle was completed, the "tom," a heavy lead weight, was dropped to pull the strings at the bottom of the purse seine tight. Fifty thousand menhaden and a few of the sharks that feed on them were trapped. Now the net was tightened around the doomed fish and all that remained was the dull, hard job of getting them from the net into the holds of the *Tideland*. But these men knew their jobs. They had been working at them for years—and their fathers before them, and their grandfathers before that.

Menhaden, very oily relatives of the herring, swim in large schools off the eastern shore of the United States. Although not fit to eat, their oil is valuable for paints, chemicals, and other uses. The rest of the fish is processed into fish meal, which is used to fatten turkeys and chicken. Many fishermen scorn the strong-smelling moss-bunker or bunker, as the menhaden is often called, but those who engage in the menhaden fishery speak of it as having "the smell of money."

The involvement of blacks with the menhaden fisheries began in 1868. That was the year old Elijah Reed, a Yankee entrepreneur, moved the operation of his menhaden boats from the Gulf of Maine to Chesapeake Bay. Finding lots of fish, he also sent south the processing equipment, boilers, and pressers that extract the oils. After Elijah's death his children carried on the work and the settlement became known as Reedsville. The move south was a lucky one, for in 1879 a shift in the water temperature of the northern waters made the menhaden disappear from the New England coast for nearly one hundred years. This drove most of the Yankee fishermen out of the menhaden fisheries and made room for the Virginia blacks, who have dominated the crew lists ever since.

In the nineteenth and early twentieth centuries the captains, engineers, "pilots," and mates were all whites, but gradually many of these jobs were opened to blacks. On the *Tideland* only Captain Edwards, descendant from a long line of whaling captains, and Kenneth Payne, pilot,

were not members of the Afro-American comunities in
Mathews County, Virginia.

Thus the coincidence of a shift of water temperature,
the availability of a labor force of strong, active men, and
the end of the Civil War and slavery combined to open a
new field to black seamen and fishermen. Strength was
needed by those who manned the purse-seine boats. The
strongest fisherman dropped the three-hundred-pound
"tom." (Today the "tom" weighs seven hundred pounds
but is hoisted with a power winch.) Sixteen men on each
boat were needed as "bunt-pullers" to tighten the net
around the fish. They also manned the oars, two men to
an oar. Two "seine men" let out the net and two "ring-
men" watched for snarls. The captain or mate acting as
boat steerer completed the boat crew. Pilot, engineers, and
cook stayed aboard the mother ship and brought it alongside the boats to hoist the fish from the net. Until the
1930's the seine boats were still propelled by oars and the
nets were tightened by hand. Steam drove the ships and
powered the donkey engines that hoisted the fish from net
to hold. Today gasoline and diesel engines have made
some of the work easier, but the nets still have to have
bulges pulled straight by muscle power and the edges
fastened to the side of the ship by the crew climbing along
the bulwarks. Strong, active, skilled men are still needed.

"Strong, active men"—the term occurs continually in
Goode's monumental study of the U.S. fisheries written
for the Government in 1879. This need for strong, active
men for outdoor work made it possible for shipowners to
justify hiring blacks instead of relying on casual white
labor. In the late 1800's blacks were considered "unsuit-

able for factory work" by many whites but were hired for all sorts of outdoor work where strength was required. As a result of this belief, menhaden factories were originally manned by whites of various nationalities, swept up from the Baltimore docks by labor contractors. This has changed as social attitudes have changed.

Menhaden ships needed crews who would work well together. Unlike the New England dory fisherman, whose share was reckoned by the number of codfish he caught personally on his line and hooks, the menhaden men's share was figured on the total fish in the nets. Hand labor was done to the tune of work song and converted hymns. The crew as a group, not the factory owner or captain, hired the cook and paid for the provisions. In 1879 Goode wrote: "The menhaden men live probably the most extravagantly of any class of fishermen and in some cases go to foolish expenditure for the table." That tradition of good food still holds. Raymond Curry, the cook of the *Tideland,* did not serve any fancy trimmings or unnecessary appetizers, but the food was certainly as fine as any served in the best restaurants of Virginia. However, there were no alcoholic drinks served aboard ship.

Breakfast was at five in the morning, lunch at 10 A.M., dinner at 2 P.M. After that it is mug-up when you're hungry, and cook your own. If food fish such as bluefish or herring accidentally got caught in the net, the crewmen put them into the icebox to take home, but fish was not served on the *Tideland.*

There never have been schools for fishermen to learn their trade, so all training is by apprenticeship. This is another reason crews tend to come from the same neighbor-

hood and social group. Fathers bring their sons, uncles
their nephews. A stranger might make a mistake that would
lose a whole netful of fish, so crew members are only taken
on when somebody vouches for their reliability and looks
to their training. The *Tideland* carried Vernel Savoy, Sr.,
as first engineer and Vernel Savoy, Jr., as second engineer.
Other crew members had joined the ship by the same
process of family recommendation.

The menhaden season is from April to the beginning of
October, if the fish are running that long. In the winter
Raymond Curry went back to his restaurant. Robert
Drummer, the second mate, was a carpenter in the off-
season, and the other crew members scattered to small
farms, to odd jobs, or sometimes to engage in oystering or
other winter fishing. The pay for menhaden fishing was
not bad, an average fisherman making in six months what
a bank clerk made for the entire year. However the hours
were long, from early dawn to dusk, and there was no
pension when physical strength gave out. There were some
good seasons and some bad ones, depending how the fish
were running. There was little risk of a menhaden ship
sinking since they never went far from shore, but few fishermen can swim if they are swept overboard or slip. Rup-
tures, rheumatism, burns from running ropes, and frac-
tures were the main risks. It was perhaps no way to get
rich, but the menhaden men preferred it to full-time farming, waiting on tables, or dock work, which were the
alternatives for most of them.

Of course, menhaden were not the only school fish pursued by Afro-Americans. Before the invention of frozen
fish and the existence of refrigerators in every farmhouse,

salted mullet was available in most southern grocery shops and general stores. These were caught by many part-time fishermen in shallow waters during October, November, and December, just when farm work was at its slowest.

"The mullet fishermen are mostly farmers," reports Goode, "turning their attention to fishing a short time only. When the fishing season arrives they proceed in gangs of four to thirty men under the leadership of a 'captain.' A seine net of seventy-five to one hundred fathoms (six feet, or approximately two meters to a fathom), two or three boats, and a limited amount of provisions, salt, barrels, and material for splitting tables constitute their outfit."

Whites as well as blacks were engaged in the mullet fisheries on the Carolina coast, while Bahamians, Cubans, and "Creoles" came over from the islands to join the mullet fishing on the Florida and Gulf coasts. Organization of the mullet camps bore the imprint of an African heritage. The election of a "captain" for a cooperative work group and the method of constructing huts with rushes or palmetto leaves are closer to African than to European culture. The actual fishing process resembles that of many parts of the North Atlantic.

When a fishing station had been selected and shelters constructed, a lookout posted on a crude tower signaled the presence of mullet close enough to be caught. One end of the net was held ashore, and the boat was launched to carry the other end around the school. Mullet are not menhaden, and catching them was more risky and difficult. The heavy surf pounding on the outer Carolina beaches made launching a boat a matter of fine judgment.

Momentary inattention, lapse of judgment, or an oar breaking at a critical moment might mean the boat filling or capsizing. The surf could easily slam an unfortunate fisherman against the sand, fracturing limbs, or the undertow could drown him. Even when the boat had fixed the net around the school of fish, mullet catching was rough. Mullet, unlike menhaden, make a real effort to escape. First they are apt to try to get under the net, but if they cannot "lift" the net, they next start jumping over the edge. To prevent the loss of too many fish, a second or third boat as well as men wading into the shallows "backed up the net." To stand in the water with pound-size fish slamming into the fishermen "made the situation anything but pleasant," as an observer wrote to Goode. When the fish were finally on the beach they had to be quickly split and salted so that the crew would be ready when another school of fish came into range. Unlike farming or factory work, lost opportunities in fishing could never be made up. Food for mullet fishers, unlike menhaden men, usually consisted of some potatoes and the fish they caught. Mullet camp huts were flimsily constructed, without windows or real furniture. Mullet catching, therefore, was seldom a preferred occupation.

Very similar to the mullet fishing in the South was the seining off the sandy beaches of New Jersey and New York's Long Island. Here too were five-men boats and shore crews to surround the fish with nets. Striped bass, weakfish, porgy, and bluefish were the catch. Crews were racially mixed from the earliest days, when the Shinnecock Indians taught the colonists how to set seine nets. Indians, blacks, and whites continued this work. The history of the town of Seaford, Long Island, tells of a black member of a seining crew who was treated as fully equal by his fellow fishermen around the turn of the century. Another black is known to be from Canarsie, and no doubt detailed study would turn up many more. Today a few seiners, descendants from Long Island's oldest families, are still netting for bass near the eastern tip of the island, but they are under increasing pressure from sports anglers who want the bass as "game" for their rods. The same kind of pressure is being applied to the menhaden fishermen by the rod-and-reelers who are after the bluefish that feed on the "bunkers."

All these activities so far mentioned are for men only. "Women's place is on shore" is the comment of most fishermen of the Atlantic coast, both black and white. In some cases they go so far as to consider the presence of a woman, even as a passenger, to be sheer bad luck. There is one form of seine fishing, however, where women did play a role.

Every spring alewives, another relative of herring, enter the mouths of southern rivers to lay their eggs. Large seines, stretched across the rivers, catch them by the thousands. Unlike the mullet camps, alewives net sites were fixed and semipermanent sheds were built for the work. Men and women worked together to haul the large nets to shore. However, setting the nets was boat work and therefore men's work. The alewives were eaten fresh, salted, or marinated, as were the herring of the northern waters. Today eating tastes have changed and both herring and alewives are likely to end up as fish meal or oil.

As individuals, blacks had been fishermen since the

earliest days of slavery. The breakup of the plantation system and the coming of railways combined to create opportunities for new part-time or full-time occupations in the fisheries. The use of seine nets and group cooperation seemed particularly suitable for the cultural background of the Afro-American. The work gangs of slavery days had re-enforced the original black experiences of West Africa. The need for "strong, active men" had prevented the race prejudices of the late 1800's and early 1900's from closing off this chance for blacks to make money.

However, unlike whaling and the Grand Banks fishery, seine netting is not "romantic" and the names of the men engaged in this work have been lost to history.

XII

Navy Men

At dawn on May 13, 1862, the lookout on board the U.S.S. *Onward,* leadship of the Union fleet blockading Charleston, South Carolina, saw a steamer bearing down through the morning mist. Immediately the drums called the crew to battle stations and the black guns swung out menacingly. The deck officer of the *Onward* grabbed his speaking trumpet and challenged the stranger: "What ship is that?"

"Steamer *Planter* come out of Charleston to join the Union fleet," was the incredible answer.

The *Onward* was taking no chances. It was the first year of the Civil War and only two months since the *Merrimac* had raised havoc among the blockaders. "Come under my lee and no tricks or we will fire into you. We are sending a boat to investigate."

Investigation soon revealed that the *Planter* was indeed quitting the hotbed of secession, Charleston, and coming out to join the Union fleet. Her escape had been planned and carried out by her black crew under the command of her slave-quartermaster, Robert Small. Aboard with him were the rest of the black crewmen and their families. Small and his fellow conspirators had waited until all the white officers had gone ashore for a party, then brought their families aboard from a hiding place on another ship. Dressing himself in the clothing of the *Planter's* white captain, he had fooled the gunners of Fort Sumter guarding the harbor. To them it looked like the *Planter* was on lawful Confederate business until it was too late to stop her trip to the blockading fleet.

Militarily the *Planter* was a valuable capture. The ship was a shallow-draft paddle wheeler, 140 feet long and 50 feet wide, big enough to transport one thousand fully equipped men. She was armed with a thirty-two-pound pivot gun and a twenty-four-pound howitzer. In addition, Small had carried away a seven-inch rifle and four smooth-bore cannons that had been placed aboard for transport to new Confederate entrenchments being built to stop the Union fleet.

Robert Small, personally, was hardly a less valuable acquisition for the Union command. The *Planter* had served as headquarters ship and dispatch boat for General Roswell Ripley, second in command at Charleston. Small, ranked as wheelman or quartermaster, had used his opportunities to note carefully not only all navigation channels of Charleston Harbor but also the position of every gun and man the Confederates had defending that vital port. He had been born on the Sea Islands and had worked as sailor, docker, and sailmaker, so he knew the coast from Beaufort, South Carolina, to Florida.

But Robert Small and his fellow crew members were

black slaves and therefore represented a political issue far outweighing the importance of their military value.

The South reacted immediately to the bold escape. "Our community was intensely agitated on Tuesday morning by the intelligence that the steamer *Planter* had been taken possession of by her colored crew and boldly run out to the blockaders. The event is scarcely credited. . . ." wrote the *Charleston Courier* on May 14, 1862.

General Robert E. Lee, acting as chief of staff to all Confederate forces, was far more explicit. "Take all steps to bring to punishment any party or parties that may be proven guilty of complicity in the affair or negligent in permitting it," he telegraphed from Richmond.

But the damage to the South was done, and for the rest of the war no Confederate captain could trust his black crew. The convenient assumption that the southern blacks did not want to be free or that blacks were too stupid to make plans and too lazy to carry them out had been proven fictitious.

In the Union lines the *Planter* affair had hardly less repercussions. In 1862 there were plenty of slaveholders in states that were loyal to the Union Government, including some of the congressmen from Kentucky, Maryland, and Missouri. They and their political friends would not like a fuss made about a black hero.

Less than five years earlier the Supreme Court, in the famous Dred Scott decision, had ruled that slaves were property, not citizens. General Butler, occupying Hampton, Virginia, for the Union, had used that ruling to coin the term "contraband" for escaped slaves. That way, he claimed, since slaves were valuable property to the rebels, it was an accepted act of war to take them away from such rebels and use them for the Union.

Cautious Commander Du Pont, although sympathetic to Small and to abolition, recognized that he had a problem. "I do not know whether, in the view of the government, the vessel will be considered a prize," he wrote to Washington, "but if so, I respectfully submit to the [Navy] Department the claims of this man Robert Small and his associates."

The abolitionists in Congress and some of the northern newspapers were not cautious. Pictures and stories about Robert Small were featured in the *New York Tribune* and *Harpers*. By May 19 a bill was rammed through congress "for the benefit of Robert Small and others." Congressman Crittenden of Kentucky clapped his hat on his head and led his fellow slaveholders out of the hall. However, in reality the bill was less bold than it looked, for the *Planter* and its guns were appraised for a mere $9,168, less than one eighth of her real value. But politically the right of escaped slaves to be classed as persons and not property was established. The term "contraband" and the subterfuges it implied had been changed by the bold act of Robert Small.

The Army and Navy needed men, so the Department of the Navy and the War Department could not afford to be cautious. Like congress, they now proceeded to treat escaped slaves as freemen but not quite as equals of whites. "Contrabands are to be enlisted but rated as boys . . . ," ordered Secretary of the Navy Welles. Secretary of War Stanton concurred: "You may turn over to the Navy any number of colored volunteers that may be required for the naval services. You are reminded that by act of congress all men received into the services are free. . . ."

Two months after Small's escape, President Lincoln submitted the first draft of the Emancipation Proclamation to his cabinet, although it was not released publicly until September and did not go into effect until January 1863. Although uncertain how much influence Small's deed had on Lincoln's decision, history records that Small was given as an argument for freeing the slaves against opposition not only in the Confederacy and the border states but even in the majority of the legislatures of New Jersey and Illinois, who passed resolutions against emancipation.

Robert Small was not through with his heroics. He had been rated as "pilot"—a civilian employee of the Navy. Transferred to the ironclad *Keokuk,* he guided that ship in the abortive naval attack on Charleston. When it was sunk by the guns of Fort Sumter, Small was rescued and transferred back to the *Planter,* still rated as pilot. The *Planter* was now operating as a civilian ship under contract to the Army. Just before Thanksgiving 1863, the *Planter* was ambushed by Confederate batteries in a narrow stream. The white captain, a New Englander, wanted to surrender, but Small would not do so. He knew the Confederates did not treat blacks as prisoners of war but would hang him and every black crew member as an object lesson. Ordering the guns of the *Planter* to return the Confederate fire, he ignored his white superior officer and ran the steamer past the battery despite a number of hits scored on his ship. The white captain hid in the steel-clad coal bunker while the battle was on. Small bolted down the hatches to keep him there until the *Planter* returned to her base. Then there could be no arguments on the facts of the case.

The cowardly white captain was dismissed and the black hero was appointed captain of the *Planter*. Robert Small, black ex-slave, was now addressed as "captain" and "master"—but in the Navy there was still no black man who was acknowledged to be "an officer and a gentleman." In the heyday of Reconstruction a black congressman did appoint a black, James Henry Conyers, as midshipman to the Naval Academy, but Conyers was dropped for academic insufficiencies in 1872.

Until the Civil War the Navy had treated black enlisted men as almost equal to whites. There were no separate quarters for blacks and no ships that were singled out as "black," unlike the Army units that were designated "colored." Black and white ate together and fought together. Only in promotion did there seem to be discrimination by skin color. If the letters written by white Navy men during the Civil War are to be trusted, there was little resentment between them and their black fellow crewmen. By the end of the war about one fourth of the seamen in the Union Navy were black, some 29,000 of them.

There were plenty of black heroes in the fleet. Robert Blake, gunboat *Marblehead,* medal of honor; Aaron Anderson, USS *Wyandonk,* medal of honor; Joachim Pearse, aboard the *Kearsage* in action against the Confederate raider *Alabama,* medal of honor. Three blacks won medals of honor for their role in the attack on Mobile: William Brown and James Mifflin on the USS *Brooklyn* and Wilson Brown on the USS *Hartford.* There were other heroic black sailors, with and without medals.

Even the Confederate navy used a significant number of blacks. There are records of black dock workers, shipbuilders, firemen, and deckhands on Confederate ships, but after Robert Small no black would ever again be trusted in a position from which he might escape to the Union forces. Small had become a symbol for those who had "voted with their feet" as well as their hearts and hands for freedom.

The Civil War was not the first conflict where blacks had served in the U.S. Navy. Although there were few official Navy ships during the Revolutionary War, as separate from privateers, surviving muster rolls show blacks aboard the *Alliance, Ranger,* and *Reprisal* in the Continental service. In the state navies, South Carolina listed Stephen Bond, George Cooper, and John Featherstone on the schooner *Defense* as blacks. The Virginia lists show Ambrose Lewis and Joseph Ranger on the galleys *Dragon* and *Jefferson.* Three "negroes" are listed on the surviving muster rolls of Robert Mullins' First Company of Marines. After the Revolution the U.S. naval forces, with their mixed crews, were in action against the Algerian pirates and the revolutionary French fleet. But the most interesting evidence of the attitude toward blacks comes from correspondence dealing with impressment, forcible recruitment, of American sailors by the British.

On June 22, 1807, the British frigate *Leopard* stopped the U.S. frigate *Chesapeake* in international waters. Acting under orders of the British admiral, the captain of the *Leopard* demanded the return of five deserters from the British warship *Melampus* who had escaped to the *Chesapeake.* Refused, the *Leopard* fired into the unprepared *Chesapeake* and forced her to surrender. Of the five sailors removed by the *Leopard,* one was an Englishman and three were American-born blacks who had been forcibly "impressed" from an American merchantman in the Mediterranean. The diplomatic correspondence that followed between the United States and England never made any distinction between white and black sailors of the *Chesapeake.* Despite the fact that four Americans were returned by the British in 1811 (the Englishman was hung), President Madison asked for a declaration of war, listing impressment among the causes for the War of 1812.

During that war the U.S. Navy built squadrons of ships to seize control of Lake Champlain and Lake Erie from the British. On Lake Erie, Captain O. H. Perry had a fleet of ten sail by July 1814 manned by four hundred sailors, "one fourth of them negroes." Perry was not happy with the composition of his crews. His letter on the subject to his superior, Commodore Chauncey, still exists: "The men that came by Mr. Chaplin were a motley set, blacks, soldiers, and boys," he wrote. "I cannot think that you saw them after they were selected. I am, however, pleased to see anything in the shape of a man."

Commodore Chauncey, having enough trouble manning his own fleet on Lake Champlain, did not think much of the complaint. "I regret that you were not pleased with the men sent you by Messrs. Chaplin and Forrest, for to my knowledge a part of them are not surpassed by any seaman in the fleet, and I have yet to learn that the color of the skin or the cut and trimmings of the coat can affect a man's qualifications or usefulness. I have nearly fifty blacks on this boat, many of them among the best of my men. . . ."

Perry was to change his opinion of blacks as sailors and

fighters. In the report of the battle he sent to the Secretary of the Navy, he spoke of the blacks: "They seemed totally insensible to danger." He also addressed a special message to his "men of color" thanking them for their services. One of the black heroes of the Battle of Lake Erie has been immortalized in a painting hung in the U.S. Capitol. It shows Cyrus Tiffany of Taunton, Massachusetts, trying to pull Perry down to a seat in the small boat in which they were transferring from the *Lawrence* to the *Niagara* under fire.

General Jackson, thanking his mixed force of sailors, soldiers, and smugglers for their service at the Battle of New Orleans, also used the term "men of color."

Despite the acknowledged heroism of the blacks during the war, official attitude toward blacks in the United States armed services was changing. In 1815 the War Department directed the discharge of all "soldiers of color as being unfit to associate with American soldiers." The Navy never subscribed to this harsh attitude, although problems in the southern ports and with southern naval officers made conditions somewhat difficult for blacks.

The Spanish-American War brought expansion and fame to the Navy. In that conflict black and white enlisted men served together. Robert Penn won a medal of honor aboard the U.S.S. *Iowa* at Santiago. John Henry Turpin was a survivor of the battleship *Maine* when she was blown up in Havana Harbor. He was listed as "bosun," a relatively high noncommissioned rank, so there must have been some opportunities for advancement for blacks in the Navy. However, there were no black commissioned officers in the Navy itself, although they served as captains in the Coast Guard and on auxiliary ships.

Michael A. Healy rose to the rank of captain in the Coast Guard, or Revenue Service as it was then called, in 1883. From 1886 to 1895 he commanded the famous steamer *Bear* in Alaskan waters. At that time, before the Klondike gold rush, Healy and his crew were just about all the law there was in the North, and the *Bear* apprehended seal poachers, brought relief to isolated villages, and arrested murderers. The job did not always make Healy popular, but there seems to be no complaint on the basis of color or race. The U.S. Coast Guard Lifeboat Station at Pea Island, North Carolina, was manned by Negroes continuously from 1880 to 1947 and rescued hundreds of mariners.

After the Spanish-American War the Navy began recruiting Filipinos to serve as mess attendants on Navy ships. In part they replaced the blacks who had practically controlled that department since before the Civil War. Although this reduced some opportunities for blacks, it broke down even further the separation of black and white aboard ships. The involvement of the United States in World War I was too short for any expansion of the role of blacks in the Navy.

World War II began for the Navy with an act of heroism by Dorie Miller, messman aboard the battleship U.S.S. *West Virginia* docked at Pearl Harbor, December 7, 1941. When the Japanese attackers blasted the *West Virginia*, Miller first helped place his mortally wounded captain under cover and then manned a machine gun. Despite the fact that Miller had never been trained to operate such a weapon, he managed to down two attacking aircraft. For his actions he was awarded the Navy Cross. Dorie Miller died when the auxiliary aircraft carrier *Liscombe Bay* was sunk by a Japanese submarine two years later.

Meanwhile the Navy was training many additional recruits in segregated *Camp Robert Small* at the Great Lakes
Training Station near Chicago. Vice Admiral Samuel L.
Gravely, Jr., now commanding the U.S. Third Fleet in the
Pacific, went through that training and recalls: "You came
to realize that you were saving America for democracy, but
not allowed to participate in the goddam thing." However,
by 1944 the Navy commissioned the first twelve black line
officers. At first the black officers were placed aboard the
sub-chaser *PC 1264* and the destroyer-escort *Mason,* which
were specifically commissioned to train black crews, but
black officers were not welcome in the officers clubs.

In 1945 Wesley A. Brown was appointed to the U.S.
Naval Academy and was the first black to graduate. In 1948
President Truman issued orders to fully integrate the entire armed forces, and slowly black officers as well as enlisted men gained acceptance and welcome in the Navy.
Today Admiral Gravely is the highest ranking black in the
Navy, but other black officers can be found anywhere from
the elite naval air arm to the submarine service. Commodore Chauncey's words of 1814 are finally coming true, that
the color of a man's skin does not affect a man's qualifications or usefulness.

Appendix:

Where to See the Black Maritime Heritage

Evidence of the black sea heritage is widely scattered, partly because there was no distinction made at sea for men of color. Photos and ships' registers of mixed crews are found in most major maritime museums. The Mariners Museum in Newport News, Virginia, the San Francisco Maritime Museum, and the Peabody Museum in Salem, Massachusetts, have many photographs of blacks engaged in the maritime profession. Crew lists kept by the Seaman's Bethel indicating complexion and country of origin of the whalers shipping out of New Bedford, photographs of colored seamen, and a half-size replica of a whaling ship are to be found in the New Bedford Whaling Museum. The original whaling ship *Charles Morgan*, on which many Cape Verdeans and blacks served, survives in Mystic Seaport, Connecticut. There are also many photos of black coopers, shipwrights, dockworkers, and sailors scattered throughout the exhibits in Mystic Seaport. The Whaling Museum of Cold Spring Harbor, New York, possesses a whaleboat, gear, and Robert Cushman Murphy's photographs of his voyage with a predominantly West Indian crew aboard the *Daisy*. There are other whaling museums with similar artifacts in Nantucket, Martha's Vineyard, Sharon, Massachusetts, Sag Harbor, and Southhampton, N.Y.

A permanent photo exhibit on the black Chesapeake oystermen is on display in Maryland's Calvert Marine Museum. The Chesapeake Bay Maritime Museum of St. Michael's, Maryland, shows blacks oyster tonging, clam dredging, shucking oysters, picking crabs, log canoe racing, and sailing a brogan in its watermen's exhibit and waterfowl exhibit and in the Dodson House. At the museum's pier is a working bugeye, a skipjack, sailing canoe, crabbing skiffs, and a large shed containing the tools of the waterman's trade.

Thirty or so skipjacks are still used on the Chesapeake. There is an annual skipjack race offshore Crisfield, Maryland, where a number of working skipjacks are regularly docked. Skipjacks can also be viewed at the Baltimore Seaport, Penn's Landing in Philadelphia, and Chandler's Wharf in Wilmington, North Carolina.

The growing number of outdoor museums with real ships give a good impression of what life and work was like aboard deepwater sailing vessels. The height and size of the yardarms of the square-riggers—the *Peking* in New York, the *Moshulu* in Philadelphia, the *Balcutha* in San Francisco, the *Star of India* in San Diego, and the *Falls of Clyde* in Honolulu—give an idea of what it meant to go aloft to trim the sails in storm rounding Cape Horn. Hugh Mulzac and many other blacks served aboard these types of vessels; colored seamen are known to have sailed aboard the *Wavertree* exhibited at the South Street Seaport Museum.

Original coasting schooners can be seen in summer sailing out of Camden and Rockland, Maine, carrying vacationers instead of cargo; there is a proposal to put one back to hauling cargo. The ninety-two-year-old coaster *Pioneer* in New York has a marine mechanics program for black and disadvantaged youth and takes visitors for a cruise in New York Harbor. There are several schooners surviving on the West Coast: in the Maritime Museum at Vancouver, at the Northwest Seaport in Kirkland, Washington, and in the San Francisco Maritime Historic Park.

Sternwheel passenger steamboats, the *Belle of Louisville* and the *Delta Queen*, still operate on the Mississippi River as excursion boats. Steam tugboats that used to tow the sailing ships out to sea and lightships can be boarded at the South Street Seaport Museum in New York; at Newport News, Virginia; and at the San Francisco Maritime Historic Park. Lightships on which Cape Verdeans actually served are located in New Bedford and Nantucket.

Replica vessels which carried negro slaves are the *Mayflower* in Plymouth, Massachusetts; the Revolutionary War privateer *Providence II* in Newport, Rhode Island; as well as the clipper *Pride of Baltimore*. The site where African slaves were first landed in the English colonies in 1619 can be visited in the reconstructed Jamestown settlement. A replica of the *Santa Maria* cruises the east coast and can be boarded by the public for a fee. A copy of the British frigate *H.M.S. Rose*, on which Negro seamen served, floats at King's Dock, Newport, while a replica of a 1778 privateer, the *Swift*, sails out of Santa Barbara, California, for hire. There is a reconstruction of the tea-ship, *Beaver*, and a memorial to Crispus Attucs in Boston.

The Museum of Science in Boston has models of Egyptian seagoing craft and other vessels on which Blacks served. The New York Metropolitan Museum of Art has original Egyptian ship models recovered from the Tomb of Mekurta (2000 B.C.) with brown-skinned clay figures harpooning fish, rowing against the wind, and hauling up a sail. In a wall painting from the Tomb of Menna (1400 B.C.) there are dark and light skinned rowers and in a facsimile of a tomb (Amenhotep) mural from 1350 B.C. there are Negroes depicted aboard the royal barge. The American Museum of Natural History displays a cast-net from Africa and indicates it is identical to one used by the Gullah-speaking Blacks of the Carolina and Georgia coasts. The Museum has life-sized African anthropological and cultural exhibits, copies of the Mexican temples and negroid statues, and a descriptive panel on the slave trade and its effects. The Chicago Museum of Science and Industry possesses a large ship model collection, including a Nile boat of 2750 B.C., a replica of the mizzenmast deck of a windjammer, and the gundeck of the U.S.S. *Constitution.*

Blacks are known to have sailed aboard the U.S.S. *Constitution* docked in Boston, the *Constellation* in Baltimore, and Perry's flagship the U.S.S. *Niagara* permanently berthed in Erie, Pennsylvania. The remains of a Confederate gunboat and a museum devoted to the Confederate Navy are located in Columbus, Georgia. The Spanish-American War cruiser *Olympia,* on which Negro messmen served, is open to the public in Philadelphia. The World War I battleship *Texas,* built at Newport News, is in Houston, Texas; World War II ships can be found in Philadelphia; Fall River, Massachusetts; Mobile, Alabama; Galveston, Texas; Wilmington, North Carolina; and Charleston, South Carolina.

In Washington, the Navy Memorial Museum has an oil painting by V. Zveg depicting blacks in the landing party for the attack on Fort Montague, Bahamas in 1776; a memorial to John Henry Turpin, who survived the explosion on the *Maine* in 1898 and the *Bennington* in 1905 and was made the first black chief petty officer in the Navy during World War I; the story and photos of Jesse Brown, the first black navy aviator to lose his life in Korea as well as three dimensional exhibits on the Barbary Wars, 1812 Lake campaigns, Civil War, and the opening of Japan. A slide show on "Black Americans in the Navy" is available as part of the Minority Opportunities Exhibit from the Exhibit Center of the Navy. An original 1776 gunboat and models of the schooner *Hannah* (1775) which harassed British transports, the tobacco ship *Brilliant* (1775) which became a Royal Navy transport, the U.S. frigate *Confederacy* captured by the British in the West Indies, the U.S. Frigate *Raleigh* also seized, the privateer *Rattlesnake* (1780), the U.S. *Constellation* (1797), the U.S. *Constitution* (1797), sloop of war *Niagara* (1813), ship of line *Delaware* (1820), the *Vincennes* of the Wilkes Exploring Expedition, Union and Confederate Ironclads, Spanish-American War cruisers, and modern warships are found in the Smithsonian Museum of History and Technology. There are also paintings of the Battle of Lake Erie, the capture of the *Guerrière*, the blockade of Tripoli, the landing of Americans in Japan; a seachest, scrimshaw and canvas bag of a seaman from New Bedford; an exhibit on Negro slavery with a reference to the Salem slave traders in Zanzibar; a Wollof cloak and a Liberian leather pouch from the American Colonization Society. The first Washington residence of Frederick Douglass houses a fine museum of African art and a permanent exhibit the "Life and Times of Frederick Douglass." The last home of Douglass, also in Washington, has his caulker's hammer and a portrait of Douglass in his twenties.

The Annapolis Naval Historical Wax Museum shows slaves being sold off the docks of Annapolis, blacks with Perry in Japan and aboard the *Lawrence* in the War of 1812. The Naval Academy has models of ships and paintings of naval actions in which black sailors were involved, in addition to the famous flag from the battle of Lake Erie with the words "Don't Give Up the Ship."

The new Afro-American Historical and Cultural Museum in Philadelphia has a model of a slave ship with a dramatic recording of the "middle passage" as experienced by a slave, a tapestry of the *Amistad* incident, a copy of the painting of Cinque and likenesses of Crispus Attucs, Paul Cuffee, James

Forten, and Frederick Douglass. There is mention of blacks coming to the New World in Egyptian times and in the Middle Ages and accompanying Columbus, Cortes, Balboa, and Pizarro; a panel on the Maroon societies, a photo of the Bush Negroes of Surinam burning out a log canoe, photographs of black crewmen aboard the Union warship *Monitor*, World War I messmen, the first Negro Waves, Marcus Garvey and the Yarmouth, and the Sun Shipyard finally opened to black workers during World War II. A life-size blowup of seaman Matthew Henson claims he was the first to reach the North Pole while Peary lay behind exhausted. The Franklin Institute in Philadelphia has a model of the *John R. Manta* and other ship models as well as a deckhouse where children can turn the wheel. The Philadelphia Maritime Museum has models and plans of slave ship clippers and operates the Portuguese barkentine *Gazela Primeiro*, the last square-rigger working in the North Atlantic, as a sail training vessel for young people of all backgrounds.

The New Haven Afro-American Historical Society has gathered a collection of thirty pictures showing black whalers, Civil War seamen, early Coast Guard sailors, and blacks in other maritime occupations, which it intends to exhibit throughout Connecticut. A memorial to Paul Cuffee is affixed to the Friends Meeting House in Westport, Massachusetts, while Cuffee's manuscripts are in the New Bedford Public Library.

The documents relating to the *Amistad* incident and the colonization of Sierra Leone and Liberia are kept at the *Amistad* Research Center in New Orleans. The Center has also the largest collection of letters and original material relating to Negro life in America, including sea chanties and riverboat work songs. The Schomburg Collection in New York has extensive newspaper clippings of the struggle for equality in the maritime professions. The South Street Seaport Museum organized the exhibit "The Black Man and the Sea" in 1974, and the Winter 1973-1974 issue of the *South Street Reporter* carried seventeen photos, sketches, and brief notes about black maritime heritage. Research on the black man and the sea has been conducted at Howard University and at the Hampton Institute. A major study of racial policies in the shipbuilding, longshore, and offshore maritime industries was completed by the Wharton School of the University of Pennsylvania in 1970. The National Maritime Historical Society, housed in the old Marine Fire House underneath the Brooklyn Bridge in New York, has an exhibit devoted to the last sailing ship to make the voyage to Africa, the *Ernestina*, and has published several articles on black seamen in its journal *Sea History*. It is hoped that the *Ernestina* will become a floating museum for the black sea heritage and will stimulate further research in the field.

Glossary

A. B.	The rating of an able-bodied seaman who performs all the basic duties aboard ship.
baleen	Proper name for whalebone, which was used for corsets in the nineteenth century.
barque	Sailing vessel with three masts; square—rigged on the fore and main and fore-and-aft-rigged on the mizzen. In the nineteenth century four- and five-masted barques of up to about 3,000 tons were built for the grain and nitrate trade to South American ports around Cape Horn.
barquentine	A vessel resembling a barque but square-rigged on the foremast only, main and mizzen being fore-and-aft-rigged.
beam	One of the transverse timbers of a ship's frame on which the decks are laid.
bilge	Nearly horizontal part of a ship's bottom where internal water collects.
boom	The pole (spar) attached to the bottom (foot) of the sail.
bo'sun (**boatswain**)	The petty officer in direct charge of sails, rigging, anchors, cables, etc., and of all work on deck. He details the crew to carry out the day-to-day work of the ship.
bowsprit	The spar projecting out from the ship's bow to which forestays are attached.

brig	A two-masted, square-rigged sailing vessel used originally for short and for coastal trading voyages and as navy training ships.
brigantine	A two-masted vessel, square-rigged on the foremast and fore-and-aft-rigged on the main mast.
bucko mate	The term applied to a mate of a sailing ship who drove his crew hard through shouting or brutality.
bunker	Compartments aboard ship for stowing coal or oil; filling or replenishing a ship's bunker is known as bunkering.
calabash	A gourd whose shell can be used for holding liquid.
contraband	Goods prohibited from entering a belligerent state by the declaration of a blockade; smuggled goods.
cordage	Ropes used in rigging a ship.
crimp	A person who delivered seamen to ships for a fee; often innkeepers who dumped drunken sailors aboard ships just before departure time.
cutter	A fast, small, decked, one-masted sailing vessel used as an auxiliary to the war fleets and in preventive service against smugglers; a steam vessel of about 2,000 tons used by the U.S. Navy and Coast Guard for coastal patrol.
derelict	Any vessel abandoned at sea.
donkey engine	Small steam engine used to furnish power for a variety of mechanical tasks aboard ship but not for propulsion.
estuary	Tidal mouth of a large river.
filibuster	Name under which buccaneers were originally known in Britain and France. Although they styled themselves privateers, they seldom carried valid papers and differed only

	from pirates in that they did not prey on ships of their own nation.
fluke	The triangular shape at the end of each arm of an anchor; the barbed head of a lance or a harpoon; the triangular parts that make up the tail of a whale.
fore-and- aft rig	Where the front edge (luff) of the sail is attached to the mast or the stay.
foc'sle	The living space for the crew in the forward part of the ship.
founder	To sink below the sea's surface.
frigate	Three-masted Navy ship armed with twenty-four to thirty-eight guns carried on a single gundeck; used as the fleet lookout, signal ship, and escort ship of a convoy or cruiser in search of privateers or slavers.
galleon	Three-masted ship, square-rigged on fore and mainmasts and lateen-rigged on the mizzen; developed by John Hawkins but used by the Spanish as their principal trading vessel and warship.
galley	The rowed fighting ship of the Mediterranean dating from 3000 B.C. but used as late as the Russo-Swedish War of 1809 in the Baltic. It usually had only one sail and could only be sailed before wind; banks of oars were its primary means of propulsion.
gunwale	The plank running around the upper edge of a ship's side.
gybe	Changing course with the wind behind, whereby the boom of the mainsail swings from one side of the ship to the other side.
impressment	Seizing men to serve in the navy in time of war.
jettison	The act of throwing goods or equipment overboard to lighten a ship in danger of sinking.

keelson	The line of timber fastening a ship's floor timbers to the keel.
ketch	A sailing vessel with two masts, the rear one (mizzen) smaller than the foremast and forward of the rudder post.
lateen	The triangular sail used on the Arabian dhow and in the Mediterranean and Upper Nile.
lighter	A barge used for the conveyance of cargo from ship to shore.
mizzen	The aftermost mast of a square-rigged sailing ship, three-masted schooner, ketch, or yawl.
mtepe	The sewn sailboat of East Africa with a bird-like prow, reed deck house, and raking mast built in the Bajun Islands of Lamu Archipelago.
point	To sail a certain angle to the wind direction.
port	The left-hand side of a vessel as seen from behind.
prize	An enemy ship captured at sea by a ship of war or a privateer and sold by the admiralty court for benefit of the crew.
quarter	The two after parts of the ship, one on each side of the centerline.
quartermaster	The ship's officer directly in charge of stowing the hold, coiling the cables, and the upkeep and use of the navigational equipment; the senior helmsman who takes over when a ship is entering or leaving port.
rake	The angle of a ship's masts, usually slanting aft.
rigging	All wires and ropes used to support the masts (standing rigging) and for hoisting, lowering, or trimming the sails (running rigging).
schooner	A sailing vessel rigged with fore-and-aft sails on her two or more masts.
seam	The narrow gap between the planks of a ship.

seine   A long, shallow net used to catch surface fish; in days of sailing navies these nets were always included in the ship's gear to provide fresh fish for the crew.

sextant   A navigational instrument that measures the angular distance of objects by means of reflection.

shallop   A light sailing vessel of about twenty-five tons, used for fishing and as a tender of men-of-war.

shipwright   A builder of wooden ships.

shoal   A submerged sandbank.

skiff   A light rowboat.

sloop   A sailing vessel with a single mast, mainsail, and one jib.

spar   A general term for any wooden support used in the rigging of a ship, such as the mast, yard, boom, and gaff.

square rig   Where the main driving sails are approximately square and laced to horizontal poles (yards) that are attached at right angles to the mast.

starboard   The right-hand side of a vessel as seen from behind.

stem   The foremost timber forming the bow of a vessel.

stern   The rear of a ship.

topsail   The sail above the mainsail on schooners or second sail in ascending order on a square-rigged ship.

trawler   A fishing vessel with a large net in the form of a bag for catching bottom fish.

tryworks   The iron pots set in brickwork to boil the oil out of the blubber of whales; "trying out."

yard   A large wooden or metal pole (spar) crossing the mast of a ship horizontally or diagonally to which the sail is attached.

Bibliography

Adams, John E. "Primitive Whaling in the West Indies." *Sea Frontiers,* Vol. XXI, No. 5 (Sept.–Oct. 1975), pp. 72–77.

Adams, Russell L. *Great Negroes Past and Present.* Chicago: Afro-American, 1963.

Africanus, Joannes Leo. *The History and Description of Africa.* London: Hakluyt Society, 1896.

Albion, Robert G. *Rise of New York Port.* New York: Appleton, 1939.

———. *Seaports South of the Sahara.* New York: Appleton, 1959.

Allen, Gardner Weld. *Our Navy and the Barbary Corsairs.* Hamden, Conn.: Archon Books, 1965.

Andrews, Roy Chapman. *Under a Lucky Star.* New York: Doubleday, 1937.

Aptheker, Herbert. *American Negro Slave Revolts.* New York: Columbia University Press, 1943.

———. (ed.). *A Documentary History of the Negro People in the United States.* New York: Citadel Press, 1974.

———. *The Negro in the American Revolution.* New York: International Publishing, 1940.

———. *To Be Free.* New York: International Publishers, 1968.

Armistead, Wilson. *A Tribute for the Negro.* Manchester, England: William Irwin, 1848.

Asbury, Herbert. *The Gangs of New York.* New York: Garden City Publishers, 1927.

Baird, Henry Carey. *General Washington and General Jackson on the Negro Soldier.* Philadelphia: H. C. Baird, 1863.

Beecher, John. *All the Brave Sailors, The Story of the Booker T. Washington.* New York: L. B. Fisher, 1945.

Beehler, William Henry. *The Cruise of the Brooklyn.* Philadelphia: J. B. Lippincott, 1885.

138   Bibliography

Belton, Bill. "The Indian Heritage of Crispus Attucks." *Negro History Bulletin*, Vol. XXXV, No. 7 (Nov. 1972), p. 149.

Bennett, Lerone, Jr. *Before the Mayflower: A History of the Negro in America*. Chicago: Johnson Publishing, 1962.

Bennett, Norman R., and George E. Brooks, Jr. *New England Merchants in Africa*. Brookline, Mass.: Boston University, 1965.

Billington, Reg Allen. "James Forten: Forgotten Abolitionist." *Negro History Bulletin*, Vol. XIII (Nov. 1949), pp. 31–36.

Biyi, E. "Story of the Kru People." *Journal of the Royal African Society*, Vol. XXIX (1929), pp. 71–77, 181–188.

Blumrosen, Alfred W. "The Newport News Agreement—One Brief Moment in the Enforcement of Equal Employment Opportunity." *Law Forum*, Fall 1968, p. 315.

Boatner, Mark. "The Negro in the American Revolution." *American History Illustrated*, Vol. IV, No. 5 (1969).

Bontemps, Arna. *Free at Last*. New York: Dodd, Mead, 1971.

Booth, Alan R. "The United States African Squadron 1843–1861," in Butler, J. (ed.), *Boston University Papers in African History*, Vol. I. Boston: Boston University, 1964, pp. 77–117.

Boyer, Richard O. *The Dark Ship*. Boston: Little, Brown, 1947.

Bracey, John H. *Black Workers and Organized Labor*. Belmont, Calif.: Wadsworth Publishing, 1971.

Bradley, Wendell P. *They Live by the Wind*. New York: Knopf, 1969.

Brawley, Benjamin. *Negro Builders and Heroes*. Chapel Hill, N.C.: University of North Carolina Press, 1937.

———. *A Social History of the American Negro*. New York. Collier, 1970.

Brewer, James H. *The Confederate Negro*. Durham, N.C.: Duke University Press, 1969.

Brewington, M. V. *Chesapeake Bay*. Cambridge, Md.: Cornell Maritime Press, 1953.

Bridaham, Lester Burbank (ed.). *New Orleans and the Bayou Country, Photographs 1880–1910 by George François Mugnier*. Barre, Mass.: Barre Publishers, 1972.

Bridge, Horatio. *Journal of an African Cruiser*. New York: Wiley and Putnam, 1845.

Broadhead, Eleanor. *A Brief History of the Negro in Salem, Mass.* Salem Committee on Racial Understanding (mimeo), 1969.

Brooks, George E., Jr. *Yankee Traders, Old Coasters and African Middlemen*. Boston: Boston University Press, 1970.

Brown, Letitia, and Elsie M. Lewis. *Washington from Banneker to Douglass*. Washington, D.C.: Smithsonian Institution, November, 1971.

Brown, Robert, *The Story of Africa and Its Explorers*. London: Cassell and Co., 1892.

Brown, William Wells. *The Negro in the American Rebellion*. Boston: Lee and Shepard, 1867.

Bullen, Frank. *The Cruise of the Cachalot*. New York: Dodd, Mead, 1948.

Bunting, W. H. *Portrait of a Port, Boston 1852–1914*. Cambridge: Belknap Press, Harvard University, 1971.

Burgess, Robert H. "Sail Still Reigns in the Caribbean." *National Fisheries Yearbook*, 1973.

———. *This Was Chesapeake Bay*. Cambridge, Md.: Cornell Maritime Press, 1963.

Burroughs, Polly. *Zeb*. Riverside, Conn.: Chatham Press, 1972.

Cable, Mary. *Black Odyssey: The Case of the Slave Ship Amistad*. New York: Viking Press, 1971.

Canot, Captain Thomas. *Adventures of an African Slaver*, Malcolm Cowley (ed.). New York: Albert and Charles Boni, 1928.

Canvet, Gaston Edouard Jules. *Les Berberes en Amerique*. Algiers: J. Bringan, 1930.

Carnes, Joshua. *Journal of a Voyage from Boston to the West Coast of Africa with a Full Description of Trading with the Natives on the Coast*. Boston: J. J. Jewett and Co., 1852.

Carse, Robert. *The Twilight of the Sailing Ships*. New York: Grosset & Dunlap, 1966.

Chapelle, Howard I. *American Small Sailing Craft*. New York: W. W. Norton, 1951.

———. *The Baltimore Clipper*. Salem, Mass.: Marine Research Institute, 1930.

Chippendale, Captain Harry Allen. *Sails and Whales*. Boston: Houghton Mifflin, 1951.

Churchill, E. P. *The Oyster and the Oyster Industry of the Atlantic and Gulf Coasts*. Washington, D.C.: U.S. Bureau of Fisheries, Doc. 890, 1920.

Cohn, Michael (ed.). *The Battle of Mobile Bay, Letters of a Sailor Participant*. Brooklyn: Brooklyn Children's Museum, 1964.

Coleman, Terry. *Going to America*. New York: Doubleday, 1973.

Comitaa, Lambros. *Fishermen and Cooperation in Rural Jamaica*. New York: Columbia University Ph.D., 1962.

Commager, Henry Steele (ed.). *Documents of American History*. 6th ed. New York: Appleton-Century-Crofts, 1958.

Conrad, Robert. *The Struggle for the Abolition of the Brazilian Slave Trade*. New York: Columbia University Ph.D., 1967.

Cooper, Joseph. *The Lost Continent, Slavery and Slave Trade in Africa*. London: Frank Cass, 1968.

Corry, Joseph. *Observations Upon the Windward Coast of Africa*. London: Frank Cass, 1968. (first ed. 1806.)

Coupland, R. *The Exploitation of East Africa 1856–1890, The Slave Trade and the Scramble*. London: Faber and Faber, 1939.

Crone, G. R. *The Voyages of Cadamosto*. London: Hakluyt Society, 1937.

Cronon, E. David. *The Story of Marcus Garvey*. Madison: University of Wisconsin Press, 1955.

Cuffee, Paul. *A Brief Account of the Settlement and Present Situation of the Colony of Sierra Leone*. New York: Samuel Wood, 1812.

Curtin, Philip D. *Africa Remembered, Narratives by West Africans from the Era of the Slave Trade*. Madison: University of Wisconsin Press, 1967.

———. "Sources of the Nineteenth Century Atlantic Slave Trade." *Journal of African History*, Vol. V (1964), pp. 185–208.

Dabbs, Edith M. *Face of an Island*. New York: Grossman Publishers, 1971.

D'Anvers, N. *Heroes of North African Discovery*. London: Marcus Ward and Co., 1877.

Davenport, William. *A Comparative Study of Two Jamaican Fishing Communities*. New Haven: Yale University Ph.D., 1956.

Davidson, Basil. *Africa in History*. New York: Macmillan, 1968.

———. *Black Mother, The Years of the African Slave Trade*. Boston: Little, Brown, 1961.

———. *A History of West Africa to the Nineteenth Century*. New York: Doubleday, 1966.

Davis, Arthur P. *A Black Diamond in Queen's Tiara*. New York: (n. p.), 1974.

Davis, Burke. *Black Heroes of the American Revolution*. New York: Harcourt, Brace, Jovanovich, 1976.

Davis, Daniel. *Struggle for Freedom.* New York: Harcourt. Brace Jovanovich, 1972.

Dean, Harry. *The Pedro Gorino. The Adventures of a Negro Sea Captain in Africa.* Boston: Houghton Mifflin, 1929.

Denman, J. *The African Squadron.* London: Mortimer, 1849.

Devereux, William Cope. *A Cruise in the Gorgon Engaged in the Suppression of the Slave Trade on the Coast of Africa.* London: Bell and Daldy, 1869.

Dobler, Lavinia, and Edgar A. Toppin. *Pioneers and Patriots.* New York: Doubleday, 1965.

Donnan, Elizabeth. *Documents Illustrative of the History of the Slave Trade to America.* New York: Octagon Books, 1969.

———. "The Slave Trade into South Carolina Before the Revolution." *American Historical Review,* Vol. XXXIII (1928), pp. 804–828.

Douglass, Frederick. *Life and Times of Frederick Douglass.* New York: Collier, 1962.

———. *Narrative of the Life of Frederick Douglass.* New York: Dolphin Books, 1963.

Dow, George. *Slave Ships and Slavery.* Port Washington, N.Y.: Kennikat Press, 1969.

Drotning, Phillip T. *Black Heroes of Our Nation's History.* New York: Washington Square Press, 1969.

DuBois, W. E. B. *The Philadelphia Negro.* Philadelphia: University of Pennsylvania, 1899.

———. *The Suppression of the African Slave Trade to the United States of America, 1638–1870.* New York: (n.p.), 1896.

Duignan, Peter, and Clarence Clendenen. *The United States and the African Slave Trade 1619–1862.* Stanford: Stanford University Press, 1963.

Duke, Marvin L. "The Navy Founds a Nation." *U.S. Naval Institute Proceedings,* September 1967, p. 68.

Dunbar, Gary S. *Historical Geography of the N.C. Outer Banks.* Baton Rouge: Louisiana State University Studies, 1958.

Ebony. *Guardian of the Pacific.* Vol. XXXII, No. 11 (Sept. 1977).

Edwards, Paul (ed.). *Equianos Travels.* New York: Praeger, 1966.

Engle, Eloise, and Arnold S. Lott. *America's Maritime Heritage.* Annapolis: Naval Institute, 1971.

Fage, J. D. "Slavery and the Slave Trade in Context of West African History." *Journal of African History,* Vol. X, No. 3 (1969), pp. 393–404.

Farrell, James A. *Sea Lanes South of the Sahara, The Story of the Farrell Lines.* New York: Newcomen Society, 1963.

Fax, Elton C. *Garvey.* New York: Dodd, Mead, 1972.

Fishel, Leslie H., and Benjamin Quarles. *The Negro American: A Documentary History.* Glenview, Ill.: Scott, Foresman, 1967.

Fisher, J. B. "Who Was Crispus Attucks?" *American Historical Record,* Vol. I (1872), p. 531.

Foner, Philip P. *Frederick Douglass.* New York: Citadel Press, 1964.

Foote, Andrew. *Africa and the American Flag.* New York: D. Appleton, 1854.

Foster, William Z. *The Negro People in American History.* New York: International Press, 1954.

Fowler, William M. *Rebels Under Sail.* New York: Scribner's, 1976.

Franklin, John Hope. *From Slavery to Freedom.* New York: Knopf, 1956.

———. *A History of Negro Americans.* New York: Knopf, 1967.

Frye, John. "The Smell of Money." *National Fisheries Yearbook,* 1973.

Fyfe, Christopher. *A History of Sierra Leone.* London: Oxford University Press, 1962.

Gibbs, C. R. "Blacks in the Union Navy." *Negro History Bulletin,* Vol. XXXVI, No. 6 (Oct. 1973), p. 137.

Glocester, S. *Discourse Delivered on the Death of James Forten.* Philadelphia: Ashmead and Co., 1843.

Goldberg, Joseph P. *The Maritime Story: A Study of Labor-Management Relations.* Cambridge: Harvard University Press, 1958.

Goldsmith-Carter, George. *Sailing Ships and Sailing Craft.* New York: Grosset & Dunlap, 1970.

Goode, Brown George. *The Fisheries and Fishing Industry of the U.S.* 2 vol. Washington, D.C.: Commission of Fisheries, 1887.

Gosse, Philip. *Hawkins: Scourge of Spain.* New York: Harper and Bros., 1930.

Graham, Shirley: *There Was Once A Slave.* New York: Messner, 1947.

Greene, Lorenzo J. "The Negro in the Armed Forces." *Negro History Bulletin,* Vol. XIV, No. 6 (1951), p. 123.

———. *The Negro in Colonial New England.* Port Washington, N.Y.: Kennikat Press, 1942.

———. *The Negro Wage Earner.* Washington, D.C.: Association for the Study of Negro Life and History, 1930.

———. "The Negro in the War of 1812 and the Civil War." *Negro History Bulletin,* March 1951, p. 133.

Greene, Robert Ewell. *Black Defenders of America.* Chicago: Johnson Publishing, 1974.

Greenfield, Sidney M. *Cape Verdeans in New England.* Paper presented at the Am. Anthro. Soc. meeting, Toronto, 1972.

Grenville, G. S. P. Freeman. *Chronology of African History.* New York: Oxford University Press, 1973.

Grimke, Charlotte Forten. *The Journal of Charlotte L. Forten.* New York: Collier, 1953.

Hakluyt, Richard. *The Principal Navigations, Voyages, Traffics and Discoveries of the English Nation.* London: Folio Society, 1970.

Haley, Neale. *The Schooner Era.* South Brunswick and New York: A. S. Barnes and Co., 1972.

Hamer, Philip M. "Great Britain, the United States and Negro Seamen Acts 1822–1848." *Journal of Southern History,* Vol. I, No. 3 (1935), p. 138.

Harris, Sheldon. "An American's Impression of Sierra Leone in 1811." *The Journal of Negro History,* Vol. XLVII, (1962), pp. 33–41.

Haynes, George E. *The Negro at Work During the World War and During Reconstruction.* Washington, D.C.: Government Printing Office, 1921.

Haywood, Carl Norman. *American Whalers and Africa.* Boston: Boston University Ph.D., 1967.

Henson, Mathew. *A Negro Explorer at the North Pole.* New York: Frederick Stokes, 1912.

Heyerdahl, Thor. *The Ra Expedition.* New York: Doubleday, 1972.

Hill, Donald R. *England I Want To Go.* Evansville: Indiana University Ph.D., 1973.

———. *The Impact of Migration on the Metropolitan and Folk Society of Carriacou, Grenada.* Vol. 54 Pt. 2 Anthro. Papers of the Am. Mus. of Nat. Hist. New York: 1977.

Hohman, Elmo Paul. *The American Whaleman.* New York: Longmans, Green, 1928.

Hornell, James. "African Bark Canoes." *Man,* 1935, p. 198.

———. *Water Transport, Origins and Early Evolution.* Plymouth, England: David and Charles, 1970.

Hourani, G. F. *Arab Seafaring in the Indian Ocean in Ancient and Medieval Times.* Princeton, N.J.: Princeton University Press, 1951.

Howard, Horatio. *A Self-Made Man: Capt. Paul Cuffee.* New Bedford, Mass.: New Bedford Standard Times Press, 1913.

Howarth, David. *Trafalgar.* New York: Galahad Books, 1969.

Howland, Chester. *Thar' She Blows.* New York: Wilfred Funk, 1951.

Hoyle, B. S. *Seaports and Development in Tropical Africa.* London: Macmillan, 1970.

Hughes, Langston. *Famous Negro Heroes of America.* New York: Dodd, Mead, 1958.

Hugill, Stan. *Sailortown.* New York: E. P. Dutton, 1967.

Hutchins, John G. B. *The American Maritime Industries and Public Policy 1789–1914.* Cambridge, Mass.: Harvard University Press, 1941.

Ikime, Obaro. *Merchant Prince of the Niger Delta.* New York: Africana Publishing, 1969.

Jackson, John W. *The Pennsylvania Navy 1775–1781.* New Brunswick, N.J.: Rutgers University, 1974.

Jackson, L. P. "Virginia Negro Soldiers and Seamen in the American Revolution." *Journal of Negro History,* Vol. XXVII (1942), p. 247.

Jeffreys, M. D. W. "Pre-Columbian Arabs in the Caribbean." *The Muslim Digest,* (Aug. 1954), p. 26.

Jensen, Vernon N. *Strife on the Waterfront.* Ithaca, N.Y.: Cornell University, 1974.

————. *Hiring of Dock Workers and Employment Practices in the Ports of New York, Liverpool, London, Rotterdam, and Marseilles.* Cambridge, Mass.: Harvard University Press, 1964.

Jewell, John H. A. *Dhows at Mombasa.* Nairobi: East African Publishing House, 1976.

Jobson, Richard. *The Golden Trade.* London: Okes, 1623.

Johnston, Brenda A. *Between the Devil and the Sea, The Life of James Forten.* New York: Harcourt Brace Jovanovich, 1974.

Jones, Charles H. *Africa, The History of Exploration and Adventure.* New York: Henry Holt, 1875.

Karasch, Mary. *The Brazilian Slaves and the Illegal Slave Trade, 1836–1851.* Madison: University of Wisconsin Ph.D., 1967.

Katz, William Loren. *Eyewitness: The Negro in American History.* New York: Pitman, 1967.

Keay, Frances Anne. "Oyster Boats of the Chesapeake." *Charities,* Vol. 17 (Oct.–March 1906–07).

Kellog, J. L. *Shell-Fish Industries.* New York: Holt, 1910.

Kendall, Charles Wye. *Private Men of War*. New York: Robert Mc-
Bride, 1932.

Klein, Herbert S. *Slavery in the Americas*. Chicago: Quadrangle
Books, 1971.

Kolb, C. F. "The Negro Colonists." *Negro History Bulletin,* (Oct.
1949), p. 16.

Kup, A. P. *A History of Sierra Leone 1400–1781*. London: Cambridge
University Press, 1962.

Laing, Alexander. *American Ships*. New York: American Heritage
Press, 1971.

Landau, Noah. "The Negro Seaman." *Negro Quarterly*, Vol. I. (1942/
43), p. 330.

Lane, Frederic C. *Ships for Victory*. Baltimore: Johns Hopkins Press,
1951.

Lang, John. *The Land of the Golden Trade*. London: T. C. Jack,
1910.

Langley, Harold. *Social Reform in the U.S. Navy 1798–1862*. Urbana:
University of Illinois Press, 1967.

———. "The Negro in the Navy and Merchant Service 1789–1860."
Journal of Negro History, Vol. LII, (October 1967), p. 275.

Leavitt, John R. *The Charles Morgan*. Mystic, Conn.: Mystic Seaport
Press, 1973.

Leca, N. *Les Pecheurs de Guet N'Dar*. Paris: Librairie Larousse, 1935.

Lee, Charles F. *Menhaden Industry—Past and Present*. Washington,
D.C.: Fishery Leaflet 412, Fish and Wildlife Service, Dept. of Interior, 1953.

Lee, Irwin. *Negro Medal of Honor Men*. New York: Dodd, Mead,
1967.

Levy, Mimi Cooper. *Whaleboat Warriors*. New York: Viking, 1963.

Lipfert, Bill, and Lisa Thurau. *The Treasures of Northport's Past*.
Northport, L.I.: Chamber of Commerce, 1977.

Littlefield, L. A. "Fitting Out a Whaler." *Old Dartmouth Historical
Sketch #14* (June 22, 1906).

Litwack, Leon F. *North of Slavery*. Chicago: University of Chicago
Press, 1961.

Logan, Rayford W. "Negro in the Quasi War 1798–1800." *Negro
History Bulletin* (March 1951), pp. 128–132.

Mannix, Daniel P., and Malcolm Cowley. *Black Cargoes: A History of
the Atlantic Slave Trade*. New York: Viking Press, 1962.

Marshall, F. Ray. *Labor in the South*. Cambridge: Harvard University Press, 1967.

———. *The Negro and Organized Labor*. New York: John Wiley, 1965.

———. "The Negro in Southern Unions." *The Negro and the American Labor Movement*, Julius Jacobsen (ed.). Garden City, N.Y.: Anchor Books, 1968.

Marszalek, John F. "The Black Man in Military History." *Negro History Bulletin*, Vol. XXXVI, No. 6 (Oct. 1973), p. 122.

Martin, Christopher. *The Amistad Affair*. London: Abelard-Schuman, 1970.

Mathews, John. *A Voyage to the River Sierra Leone*. London: B. White, 1788.

Mauny, Raymond. "Navigation sur les cotes du Sahara pendant l'antiquité." *Revue des Etudes Anciennes*, Vol. LVII, No. 1 (Jan. 1955), p. 92.

McHugh, J. L. *Fishery and Fishery Resources of New York Bight*. NOAA Technical Report, National Maritime Fisheries Services Circular No. 401 (March 1977).

McLeod, John. *A Voyage to Africa*. London: John Murray, 1820.

McPherson, James M. *The Negro's Civil War*. New York: Pantheon, 1965.

Mellin, Gilbert Myer. *The Mississippi Shipping Company (Delta Line); A Case Study in the Development of Gulf Coast-South American and West African Shipping 1919–1953*. New Orleans: 1955.

Minton, Henry. *Early History of Negroes in Business in Philadelphia*. Nashville, Tenn.: A.M.E.S.S. Union, 1913.

Mitchell, Joseph. "Mr. Hunter's Grave." *The New Yorker*, Sept. 22, 1956.

Montefiore, J. *An Authentic Account of an Expedition to Sierra Leone*. London: J. Johnson, 1794.

Morgan, Charles S. "The New England Coastal Schooners." *The American Neptune*, Pictorial Supplement V. Salem, Mass.: Peabody Museum, 1963.

Morison, Samuel Eliot. *Builders of the Bay Colony*. Boston: Houghton Mifflin, 1930.

———. *The Caribbean as Columbus Saw It*. Boston: Little, Brown, 1964.

——. *The European Discovery of America.* New York: Oxford University Press, 1974.

——. *The Maritime History of Massachusetts.* Boston: Houghton Mifflin, 1961.

Morsbach, Mabel. *The Negro in American Life.* New York: Harcourt Brace, 1967.

Mueller, William R. "Negro in the Navy" *Social Forces,* Vol. 24, Oct. 1945, p. 110.

Mulzac, Hugh. *A Star to Steer By.* New York: International Publishers, 1972.

Murdock, George P. *Africa, Its Peoples and Their Cultures.* New York: McGraw-Hill, 1959.

Murphy, Robert Cushman. *A Dead Whale or a Stove Boat.* Boston: Houghton Mifflin, 1967.

Nell, William C. *The Colored Patriots of the American Revolution.* Boston: Robert F. Wallcut, 1855.

Nell, William C. *Services of Colored Americans in the Wars of 1776 and 1812.* Boston: 1851.

Nelson, Lt. Dennis Denmark. *The Integration of the Negro into the U.S. Navy 1776–1947.* New York: Farrar, Straus and Young, 1951.

——. "Recent Trends in Naval Racial Policies." *Negro History Bulletin* (Oct. 1951), pp. 8–11.

Northrup, Herbert R. "The New Orleans Longshoreman." *Political Science Quarterly,* Vol. LVII (Dec. 1942), p. 527.

——. *Organized Labor and the Negro.* New York: Harper, 1944.

——, and Richard L. Rowan. *The Negro and Employment Opportunity.* Ann Arbor: University of Michigan, 1965.

Ocansey, John. *African Trading or Trials of William Ocansey.* Liverpool: James Looney, 1881.

Ogilby, John. *Africa: Description of Egypt, Barbary, Lybia, Land of Negroes, Guinea, Aethiopia and Abyssinia.* London: Thomas Johnson, 1670.

Oleson, Russ. "Sharp Spotters, Skilled Boatmen, Load Up on Porgies off Florida." *National Fisheries Yearbook,* 1976.

Olsen, Peter. "The Negro Maritime Worker and the Sea." *Negro History Bulletin,* Vol. XXXIV (Feb. 1971), p. 40.

Ovington, Mary White. *Half a Man: The Status of the Negro in New York City.* New York: Schocken Books, 1969.

Owen, William FitzWilliam. *Narratives of Voyages to Explore the*

Shores of Africa, Arabia and Madagascar. New York: J. and J. Harper, 1833.

Paine, Ralph D. *Ships and Sailors of Old Salem.* Boston: Charles E. Lauriet, (n.d.).

Pawson, Michael, and David Buisseret. *Port Royal, Jamaica.* Oxford: Clarendon Press, 1975.

Perer, Richard. *Yankees and Creoles.* London: Longmans, Green and Co., 1968.

Petrides, Bette. "The Swahili: East Africa's Maritime People." *Oceans,* Vol. VIII, No. 1 (Jan. 1975), pp. 26–31.

Pinchbeck, Raymond B. *The Virginia Negro Artisan and Tradesman.* Richmond: William Byrd Press, 1926.

Pope-Hennessy, James. *Sins of the Fathers: A Study of the Atlantic Slave Traders 1441–1807.* New York: Knopf, 1968.

Priestley, Margaret. *West African Trade and Coast Society.* London: Oxford University Press, 1969.

Purdon, Eric. *Black Company: The Story of Subchaser 1264.* Washington: Robert Luce, 1972.

Quarles, Benjamin. *The Negro in the Making of America.* New York: Collier Books, 1974.

———. *The Negro in the Civil War.* Boston: Little, Brown, 1953.

———. *The Negro in the American Revolution.* Chapel Hill: University of North Carolina Press, 1961.

Randier, Jean. *Men and Ships.* New York: David McKay, 1969.

Raskin, Bernard. *On a True Course.* Washington, D.C.: Merkle Press, 1967.

Reddick, L. B. "The Negro in the U.S. Navy During World War II." *Journal of Negro History* (April 1947), p. 201.

Reid, Ira De A. *Negro Membership in American Labor Unions.* New York: National Urban League, 1930.

Robertson, E. Arnot. *The Spanish Town Papers.* London: Cresset Press, 1959.

Rosenman, M. "Negro and the Military." *Crisis,* Vol. 74 (May 1967), pp. 196–199.

Rubin, Lester, and William S. Swift. *Negro Employment in the Maritime Industries.* Philadelphia: The Wharton School Industrial Research Unit, University of Pennsylvania, 1974.

Rubin, Vera and Arthur Tuden. *Comparative Perspectives on Slavery in New World Plantation Societies.* New York: New York Academy of Sciences, 1977.

Ruchames, Louis. *Race, Jobs and Politics: Story of the FEPC.* New York: Columbia University Press, 1953.

Russel, Maud. *Men Along the Shore: The ILA and Its History.* New York: Brussel and Brussel, 1966.

Salvador, George. *The Black Yankee.* New Bedford: Reynalds-De-Walt, 1969.

Sanderson, Ivan T. *Follow the Whale.* Boston: Little, Brown, 1956.

Sankore, Shelby. "The Negro in California History." *Negro Digest* (Feb. 1966), p. 42.

Saugnier. *Voyages to the Coast of Africa: An Account of the Slave Trade as Carried on at Senegal and Galam.* London: G. G. J. and J. Robinson, 1792.

Scammon, Charles M. *The American Whale Fishery.* New York: G. B. Putnam, 1874.

Schmitt, Frederick P. *Whale Watch.* Cold Spring Harbor, L.I.: Whaling Museum Society, 1972.

Schneider, Gail. *The Clay Pit Pond Area of Staten Island, N.Y.* Staten Island, N.Y.: Institute of Arts and Sciences, 1977.

Schoenfeld, Seymour. *The Negro in the Armed Forces.* Washington, D.C.: Associated Publishers, 1945.

Schuyler, Robert L. "Archeology of New York City Metropolis." *The Bulletin of the N.Y. State Archeo. Soc.,* No. 69 (March 1977).

Schwerin, Karl. "Winds Across the Atlantic." *Meso-American Studies,* No. 6

Shapiro, Sidney (ed.). *Our Changing Fisheries.* Washington, D.C.: National Marine Fisheries Service, Dept. of Commerce, 1971.

Sherwood, Henry Noble. "Paul Cuffee." *The Journal of Negro History,* Vol. VIII (1923), p. 206.

Shewan, Andrew. *The Great Days of Sail.* Boston: Houghton Mifflin, 1927.

Sitkoff, Harvard. "Racial Militancy and Interracial Violence in the Second World War." *Journal of American History,* Vol. LVII, No. 3, p. 672.

Smith, G. Elliot. "Ships as Evidence of the Migration of Early Cultures." *Journal of the Manchester Egyptian and Oriental Society* (1916), pp. 63–102.

Smith, Hugh M. "America's Surpassing Fisheries." *National Geographic,* Vol. XXIX, No. 6 (June 1916).

Smith, William. *A New Voyage to Guinea.* London: Frank Cass reprint, 1967.

Spero, Sterling D., and Abram L. Harris. *The Black Worker.* New York: Columbia University Press, 1931.

Stackpole, Edouard A. *The Sea Hunters: New England Whalemen During Two Centuries 1635–1835.* New York: J. B. Lippincott, 1953.

Starobin, Robert S. *Industrial Slavery in the Old South.* New York: Oxford University Press, 1970.

Sterling, Dorothy. *Captain of the Planter.* Garden City, N.Y.: Doubleday, 1958.

Sterling, Philip, and Rayford Logan. *Four Took Freedom.* New York: Doubleday, 1967.

Still, William N., Jr. "Facilities for the Construction of War Vessels in the Confederacy." *Journal of Southern History,* Vol. XXXI (1965), p. 285.

Stillman, Richard. *Integration of the Negro in the U.S. Armed Forces.* New York: Praeger, 1968.

Strick, Lisa W. *The Black Presence in the Era of the American Revolution 1770–1800.* Washington, D.C.: Education Dept., National Portrait Gallery, Smithsonian Institution, 1973.

Stuckey, S. "Remembering Denmark Vesey." *Negro Digest,* Vol. 15 (Feb. 1966), pp. 28–41.

Swann, Alfred. *Fighting the Slave Hunters in Central Africa.* Philadelphia: J. B. Lippincott, 1910.

Sweeney, William A. *History of the American Negro in the Great War.* Chicago: Cuneo-Henneberry Co., 1919.

Teixeira da Mota, A. "As Rotas Maritimas Portuguesas No Atlantico de Meadow do Seculo XV Ao Penultimo Quartel do Seculo XVI." *Do Tempo e Da Historia* (Lisbon), Vol. III (1970), pp. 13–33.

Thacher, John Boyd. *Christopher Columbus: His Life, His Work, His Remains.* New York: G. P. Putnam Sons, 1903.

Tindall, George B. *South Carolina Negroes 1877–1900.* Baton Rouge: Louisiana State University Press, 1966.

Tompkins, E. Berkeley. "Black Ahab: William T. Shorey, Whaling Master." *California Quarterly,* Vol. I (1974).

Townsend, Cyrus Brady. *Commerce and Conquest in East Africa with Reference to Salem Trade with Zanzibar.* Salem, Mass.: Essex Institute, 1950.

Tyack, David Bruce. *Cape Verdean Immigration into the U.S.* Cambridge: Harvard University Ms. Thesis, 1952.

U.S. Bureau of Naval Personnel. "The Negro in the Navy." Washington, D.C.: 1947.

U.S. Department of Defense, Office of the Assistant Secretary. *Integration and the Negro Officer in the Armed Forces of the United States.* Washington, D.C.: March 1962.

U.S. Naval History Division. *Naval Documents of the American Revolution.* Washington: Government Printing Office, 1964–.

U.S. Office of Naval Records and Library. *Naval Documents Related to the Quasi-war between the U.S. and France.* Washington: Government Printing Office, 1935–38.

———. *Naval Documents related to the United States Wars with the Barbary Powers.* Washington: Government Printing Office, 1939–44.

———. *Official Records of the Union and Confederate Navies in the War of the Rebellion.* Washington: Government Printing Office, 1894–1922.

U.S. President's Committee on Equality of Treatment and Opportunity in the Armed Services. *Freedom to serve, equality of treatment and opportunity in the Armed Services.* Washington: Government Printing Office, 1950.

Van Sertima, Ivan. *They Came Before Columbus.* New York: Random House, 1976.

Verrill, A. E. *The Bermuda Islands.* New Haven: privately printed, 1902.

———. *The Real Story of the Pirate.* New York: D. Appleton, 1923.

Villiers, Alan. *Sons of Sinbad.* New York: Scribner's, 1940.

———. *Vanished Fleets.* New York: Henry Holt, 1931.

Ward, W. E. F. *The Royal Navy and the Slavers: The Suppression of the Atlantic Slave Trade.* New York: Schocken Books, 1970.

Warner, William W. *Beautiful Swimmers.* New York: Little, Brown, 1976.

Wartis, Helen. "Shelter Island and Barbados." *Long Island Forum.* (Dec. 1972).

Wasson, George S. *Sailing Days on the Penobscot.* New York: W. W. Norton, 1949.

Weaver, Robert C. "Racial Employment Trends in National Defense." *Phylon,* Vol. III (1942), p. 22.

———. "Negro Labor Since 1929." *Race Prejudice and Discrimination: Readings in Intergroup Relations in the United States,* Arnold Rose (ed.). New York: Knopf, 1951.

Wendt, Lloyd. "The Navy's Debt to the Negro." *Negro Digest* (Sept. 1949), pp. 71–75.

——. "Negro Sailors in World War II." *Negro Digest* (Feb. 1948), p. 82.

Wesley, Charles H. *Negro Labor in the United States 1850–1925.* New York: Vanguard Press, 1927.

——. "Organized Labor and the Negro." *Afro-American History, Past and Present.* New York: Scribner's, 1971.

Wharton, James. *The Bounty of the Chesapeake.* Richmond: Virginia 350th Anniversary Celebration Corp., 1957.

Wharton, Vernon Lane. *The Negro in Mississippi 1865–1890.* New York: Harper, 1965.

Wheeler, Richard. *In Pirate Waters.* New York: Thomas Y. Crowell, 1969.

Whitman, Alden. "Hugh N. Mulzac, Mariner, Dies." *New York Times* (Feb. 1, 1971), p. 34.

Wiener, Leo. *Africa and the Discovery of America.* Philadelphia: Innes and Sons, 1920.

Williams, George Washington. *History of the Negro Race in America.* New York: G. P. Putnam, 1883.

——. *A History of the Negro Troops in the War of Rebellion.* New York: Harper, 1888.

Williams, Gomer. *History of the Liverpool Privateers and Account of the Liverpool Slave Trade.* London: 1897.

Williams, James H. *Blow the Man Down.* New York: E. P. Dutton, 1959.

Wilson, Mitchell. *American Science and Invention.* New York: Simon and Schuster, 1954.

Wilson, Ruth D. "Segregation in the Navy." *Crisis* (Nov. 1955), pp. 517–520.

Works Progress Administration, Savannah Unit, Georgia Writers Project. *Drums and Shadows.* Garden City, N.Y.: Anchor Books, Doubleday, 1972 (first pub. 1936).

Wright, R. R. "Negro Companions of the Spanish Explorers." *American Anthropologist,* Vol. IV (1902), p. 217.

Zimmerman, James Fulton. *Impressment of American Seamen.* New York: Kennikat Press reprint, originally pub. 1925.

Zobel, Hiller B. *The Boston Massacre.* New York: W. W. Norton, 1970.

Index

153